Oracle E-Business Suite Upgrades & Implementations

StreetSmarts® E-Business Suite Performance Monitoring

oracle applications &
technology consulting

Project Management, Technical
and Functional Experts
Guiding You Down the Road to Success!

Version 2.0 Bill Dunham and Michael Barone

Published by Oracle Applications and Technology Consulting (OATC)

Jamison Park
3725 Grandbridge Drive
Apex, NC, USA 27539
(919) 326-3962

Current Edition : 3/23/2017

www.oatcinc.com
Twitter : @OATCInc
LinkedIn: OATC, Inc.
Facebook: OATC, Inc.

Oracle is a registered trademark of Oracle Corporation.

Other trade and service marks are the property of their respective owners.

Cover photo taken by Mary Dunham.

All proceeds from the sale of this book will go to the Make-A-Wish Foundation.

Table of Contents

PREFACE

WHO WROTE THE *E-BUSINESS SUITE PERFORMANCE MONITORING* BOOK?

OATC, Oracle Applications and Technology Consulting, provides some of the most experienced, professional and competent consultants in the industry. We have sterling project references and experiences with many Oracle Applications and Technology projects. Below are some highlights of our expertise:

- Over 20 years' experience with Oracle technology
- Over 20 years' experience with Oracle EBS Applications
- Many Oracle EBS Application Implementations and Upgrades (MPL7→E-Business9, E-Business10, E-Business11, E-Business12)
- Upgrade Assessments *(questionnaire and script oriented, low cost analysis and feedback)*
- CEMLI (<u>C</u>ustomizations, <u>E</u>xtensions, <u>M</u>odfications, <u>L</u>ocations and <u>I</u>ntegrations/<u>I</u>ntefaces) Assessments
- Project Health Checks
- Custom Integration Projects
- Oracle EBS Applications Server Sizing and Recommendations
- Enhancing Oracle EBS Applications investment by utilizing more features and functionality of products purchased (a common problem)
- Superior Project Management and CRP Method
- Experienced Functional, Technical Developers and Database Administrators
- Remote Oracle EBS Application Services (Functional, Technical Developers, and Database Administrators)
- Remote Oracle EBS Applications and Database Monitoring & Support
- Our clients tell us we are really good ☺

We – Bill Dunham and Michael Barone – decided to share our hard-won knowledge with the Oracle EBS user community by writing this book, and the *StreetSmarts*® series. *E-Business Suite Performance Monitoring* is the third in the series; it's a collection of very useful Oracle seeded E-Business Suite performance monitoring screens, steps and procedures for your technical team members and super users.

We have perfected our E-Business Suite Performance Monitoring procedures at all of our client-sites, and they've proven very useful to us and our clients over many years on many Oracle E-Business Suite releases and versions.

This book describes and documents the quick and easy procedures that are available to your E-Business Suite DBA, SysAdmin, Super Users and Functional SME (Subject Matter Experts) using Oracle Application Manager's Dashboard to see Database Sessions, E-Business Suite Forms, and E-Business Suite Concurrent Requests.

E-BUSINESS SUITE PERFORMANCE MONITORING – WHAT IS IT ALL ABOUT?

The StreetSmarts® E-Business Suite Performance Monitoring scripts are a series of E-Business Suite Navigation, Responsibility and Screen Selections that display the E-Business Suite Database Sessions, E-Business Suite Forms Sessions and Concurrent Request Sessions.

These StreetSmarts® E-Business Suite Performance Monitoring procedures are designed to assist System Administrators, Database Administrators, or really any IS/IT personnel to identify, isolate, insulate, trace and even terminate E-Business Suite Database Sessions, E-Business Suite Forms Sessions and Concurrent Request Sessions – quickly, easily and accurately.

MORE STREETSMARTS® E-BUSINESS SUITE PERFORMANCE MONITORING TO COME!

We already have more ideas percolating, so stay tuned for updated versions of this book.

After reviewing these StreetSmarts® E-Business Suite Performance Monitoring procedures, you may scratch your head and say "*I have E-Business Suite performance monitoring procedures just like that, or even better ones that I'd like to share!*" If you would like to contribute E-Business Suite performance monitoring procedures to us for inclusion in the next version of this book, please email us at books@oatcinc.com. Please include your contact information, a brief description of your suggested E-Business Suite performance monitoring details and sample output. We will review and confirm that your procedure(s) works as planned and provide feedback on its inclusion in the next version – we will certainly give credit where credit is due!

P.S. We're pretty busy doing our day jobs, so we can't make guarantees, but we do love a challenge therefore please send-in those E-Business Suite performance monitoring requests!

You can also download this book from our website:
http://www.oatcinc.com/resources/publications-links.

Subscribe to our blog so you'll be the first to know when our next version
of *StreetSmarts*® *E-Business Suite Performance Monitoring* is available.

CHAPTER 1
E-BUSINESS SUITE 11I TO 12 ARCHITECTURE
OVERVIEW

Oracle's 11i to 12.2 Architecture includes three distinct Technology Stacks: The **Client-PC Technology Stack**, the **Application Technology Stack** and the **Database Technology Stack.**

Imagine the different hardware platforms, software versions, technology stacks integration and protocols needed to transition your desired electronic-data from the Oracle E-Business Suite **Database** to the Oracle E-Business Suite **Applications Tier** to the friendly-user sitting in front of a **Client PC.** Now imagine the skills needed to monitor, trace or even terminate a users-activity that spans all three of these stacks and you can begin to see the challenge.

Thankfully, Oracle E-Business Suite has designed and built-in utilities we can use to monitor and trace a runaway database session or an orphaned forms-session or a long-running concurrent-request.

Client-PC Technology Stack:
Windows-PCs or Mac-IOS:
Java, Mobile-Devices, Web-Browsers (Internet Explorer or Safari or FireFox)

Applications Technology Stack:

E-Business Suite 11i
JSERV (Java Servlet Engine)
JSP   (Java Server Page)
           Controls the content of Web Pages through the
           use of Servlets.
BC4J   (Business Containers for Java)
UIX   (User Interface XML) User Presentation Layer.
           Framework for Web Application technologies.
BI-Publisher and
Oracle-Forms

E-Business Suite 12.1
OC4J (Oracle Container for Java Servlet Engine)
oacore   **Oracle Application Core Technology**
forms   **Oracle Professional Forms**
OAFM   **Oracle Application Web Services**

JSP   (Java Server Page)
           Controls the content of Web Pages through the
           use of Servlets.
BC4J   (Business Containers for Java)
UIX   (User Interface XML) User Presentation Layer.
           Framework for Web Application technologies.
BI-Publisher and
Oracle-Forms

E-Business Suite 12.2
WebLogic Server
oacore   **Oracle Application Core Technology**
forms   **Oracle Professional Forms**
OAFM   **Oracle Application Web Services**

JSP   (Java Server Page)
           Controls the content of Web Pages through the
           use of Servlets.

BC4J   (Business Containers for Java)
UIX   (User Interface XML) User Presentation Layer.
           Framework for Web Application technologies.

BI-Publisher and
Oracle-Forms

Database Technology Stack:

Oracle Database 10g,
Oracle Database 11g or
Oracle Database 12c

ORACLE E-BUSINESS SUITE 11I THREE TIER ARCHITECTURE

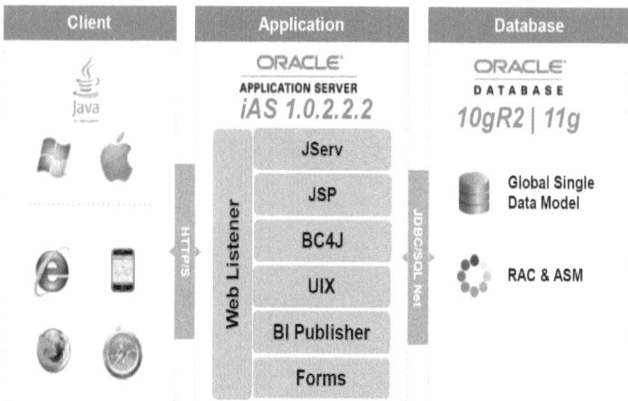

Figure 1 - Oracle Corporation Documentation, E-Business Suite Release 11i Three Tier Architecture

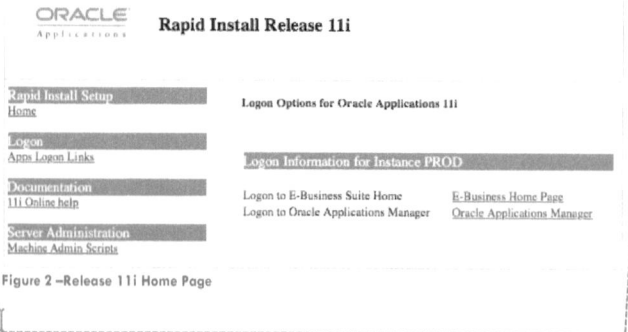

Figure 2 —Release 11i Home Page

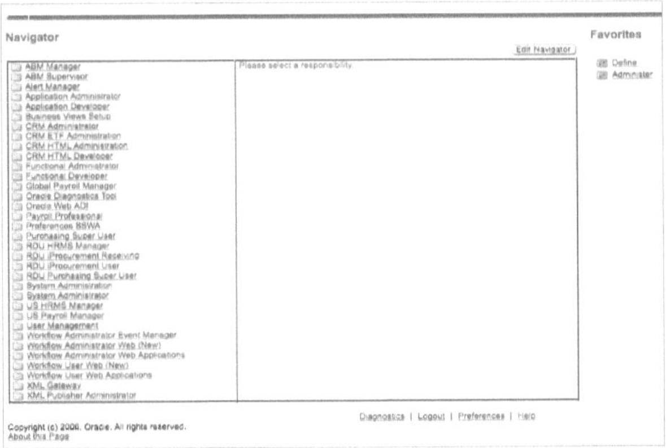

Comment [B]: redo this screenshot

Figure 3 – Release 11i Main Menu screen

ORACLE E-BUSINESS SUITE 12.1 THREE TIER ARCHITECTURE

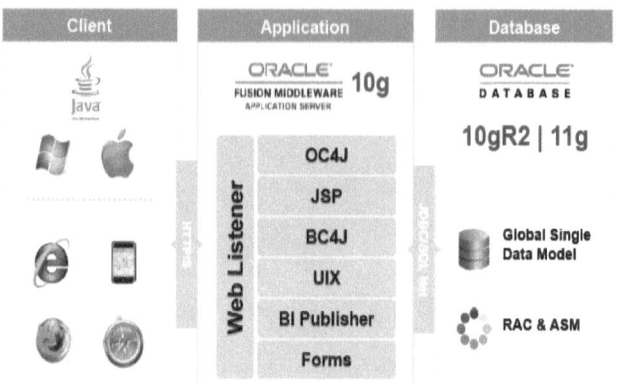

Figure 4 – Oracle Corporation, E-Business Suite Release 12.1 Three Tier Architecture

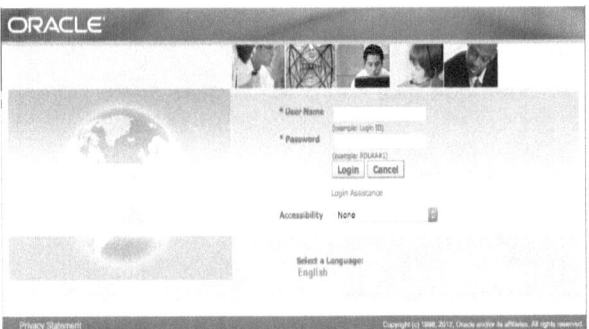

Figure 5 – Release 12.1.3 Login Screen

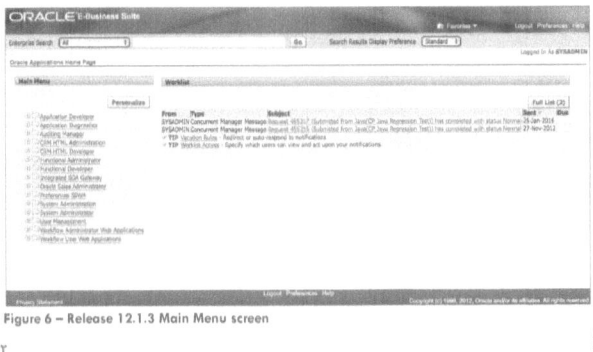

Figure 6 – Release 12.1.3 Main Menu screen

Comment [B]: redo this screen shot . When you do the screenshot, reformat the screen and make it narrower so that it will look bigger in the book and be easier to read

ORACLE E-BUSINESS SUITE 12.2 THREE TIER ARCHITECTURE

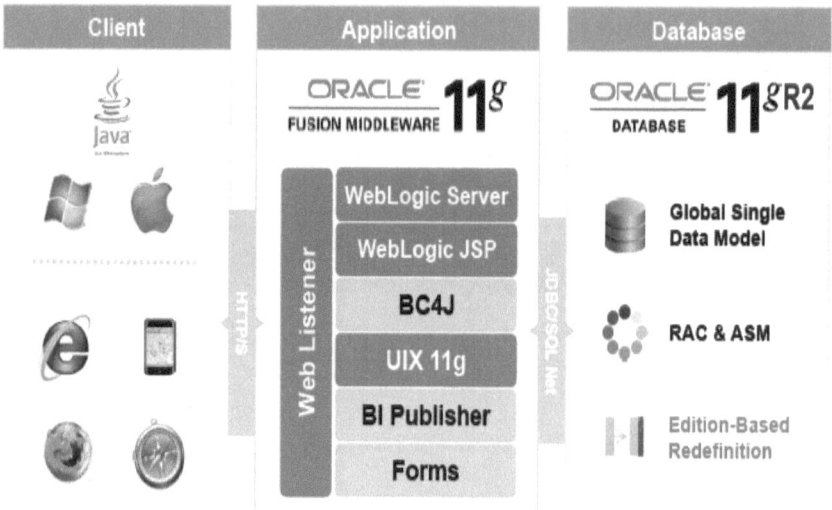

Figure 7 - Oracle Corporation, E-Business Suite Release 12.2 Three Tier Architecture

Dual File System

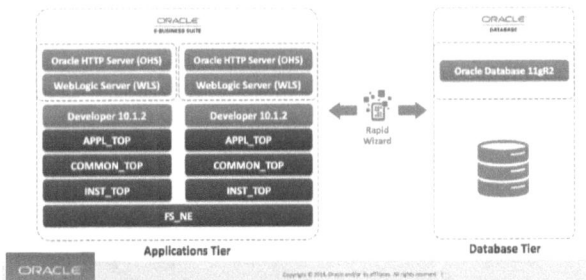

Figure 8 - Oracle Corporation, Release 12.2 Dual File System

> **Comment [B]:** Is RDU one of your customer's logos?

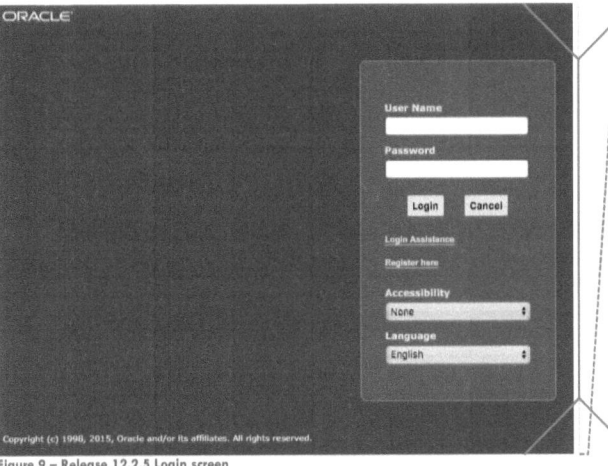

Figure 9 – Release 12.2.5 Login screen

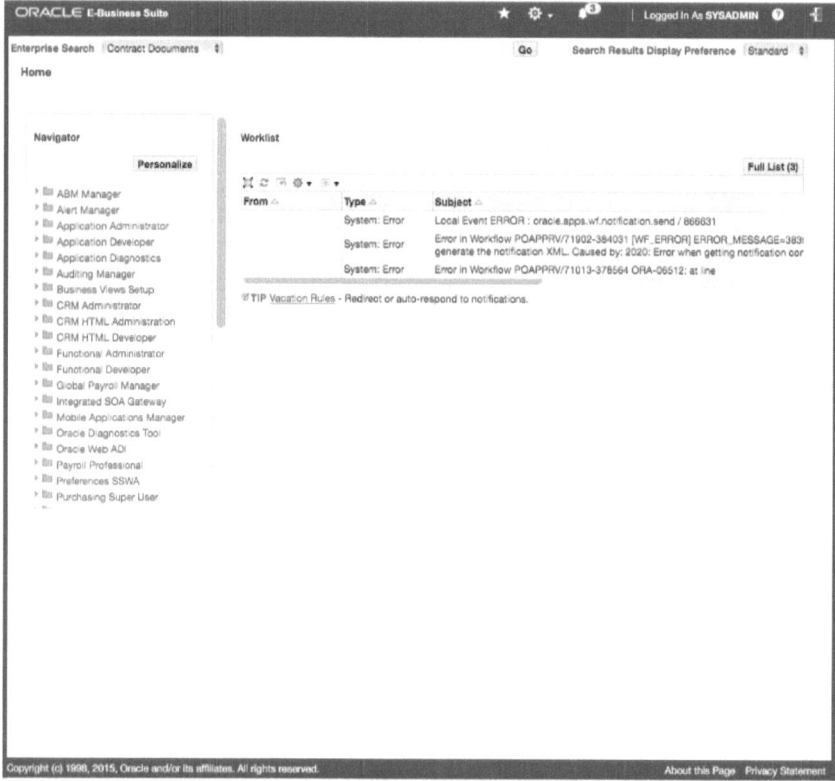

Figure 10 – Release 12.2.5 Main Menu screen

CHAPTER 2
E-BUSINESS SUITE 11I, 12.1, 12.2
PERFORMANCE MONITORING

OAM: Oracle Application Manager is an Oracle E-Business Suite seeded Responsibility. The Oracle Application Manager seeded Performance Monitoring Screens can be used to monitor, trace and terminate:

> Oracle E-Business Suite Database Sessions
> Oracle E-Business Suite Forms Sessions
> Oracle E-Business Suite Concurrent Processing Sessions.

Special Note:

- Since the E-Business Suite ICX (Internet Connections) are recorded in the ICX Tables, you can examine the ICX Connections that are current and/or historical. Additionally, the ICX history is available until the Concurrent Request: *Purge Inactive Sessions* is executed and the ICX activity is purged.

- The Forms-Connections, on the other hand, are only available when they are active. So, when a Forms User disconnects, the form information will no longer show a User with an open Forms Session.

- **Profile Options**
  Sign-On:Audit Level must be set to 'FORM' at the SITE level.

  The following procedure can be executed to display and update the Profile Option: SignOn Audit Level.

  Inserting/Updating Oracle E-Business Suite Profile-Value Options:
    Traditional Oracle Forms:
      System Administrator <Responsibility> → Profile Values
    -or-

  OA-Framework – Java-Screen: (New)
    Functional Administrator <Responsibility>
      Core Services <Menu Bar> → Profiles <Menu Tab>
        <Update> Profile Value -- Pencil-Icon
        <Create Lookup Type> -- Insert New Profile Option Value

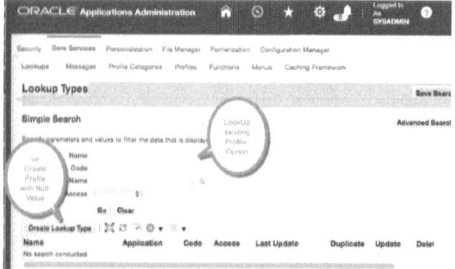

  Alternatively, the following SQL-Query can be used to identify the E-Business Suite SignOn Audit Level Profile Option Value.

Special Note: (Continued)

```
SELECT      ptl.user_profile_option_name   upname,
            pro.profile_option_name        pvname,
            DECODE(val.level_id,
            10001, 'Site',
            10002, 'Application',
            10003, 'Responsibility',
            10004, 'User',
            10005, 'Server',
            10007, 'SERVRESP',
            'UnDef')                    lvlset,
            DECODE(to_char(val.level_id),
            '10001', '',
            '10002', app.application_short_name,
            '10003', rsp.responsibility_key,
            '10005', svr.node_name,
            '10006', org.name,
            '10004', usr.user_name,
            '10007', 'Serv/resp',
             'UnDef')                      vcntxt,
            TO_CHAR(val.last_update_date,'DD-MON-RR') vupdat,
            val.profile_option_value        vvalue
    FROM    fnd_profile_options             pro,
            fnd_profile_option_values       val,
            fnd_profile_options_tl ptl,
            fnd_user                        usr,
            fnd_application                 app,
            fnd_responsibility              rsp,
            fnd_nodes                       svr,
            hr_operating_units              org
    WHERE   pro.profile_option_id = val.profile_option_id (+)
      AND   pro.profile_option_name = ptl.profile_option_name
      AND   ptl.language          = 'US'
      AND   upper(ptl.user_profile_option_name) like
            upper('%Sign-On:Audit Level%')
      AND    usr.user_id (+)              = val.level_value
      AND    rsp.application_id (+)      =
             val.level_value_application_id
      AND    rsp.responsibility_id (+) = val.level_value
      AND    app.application_id (+)     = val.level_value
      AND    svr.node_id (+)            = val.level_value
      AND    org.organization_id (+)    = val.level_value
    ORDER BY 1,3,4;
```

User Profile Name	Profile Name	Profile Level	Context	Last Update Date	Profile Value
Sign-On:Audit Level	SIGNONAUDI T:LEVEL	Site		16-AUG-02	D

Note: Sign-On:Audit Level **Profile-Value: D = Form.**

CHAPTER 3
E-BUSINESS SUITE 11I, 12.1, 12.2 -- OAM PERFORMANCE MONITORING – DATABASE SESSIONS

OAM: Oracle Application Manager is an Oracle E-Business Suite seeded Responsibility. The Oracle Application Manager Seeded Performance Monitoring Screens can be used to monitor, trace and terminate Oracle E-Business Suite Database Sessions.

Special Note:

- Since the E-Business Suite ICX (Internet Connections) are recorded in the ICX Tables, you can examine the ICX Connections that are current and/or historical. Additionally, the ICX history is available until the Concurrent Request: **Purge Inactive Sessions** is executed and the ICX activity is purged.

- The Forms-Connections, on the other hand, are only available when they are active. So, when a Forms User disconnects, the form information will no longer show a User with an open Forms Session.

- **Profile Options**
  Sign-On:Audit Level **must be set to** 'FORM' **at the** SITE **level.**

  The following procedure can be execute to display and update the Profile Option: SignOn Audit Level.

  Inserting/Updating Oracle E-Business Suite Profile-Value Options:
    Traditional Oracle Forms:
      System Administrator <Responsibility> → Profile Values
    -or-

  OA-Framework – Java-Screen: (New)
    Functional Administrator <Responsibility>
      Core Services <Menu Bar> → Profiles <Menu Tab>
      <Update> Profile Value -- Pencil-Icon
      <Create Lookup Type> -- Insert New Profile Option Value

  Alternatively, the following SQL-Query can be used to identify the E-Business Suite SignOn Audit Level Profile Option Value.

Special Note: (Continued)

```
SELECT     ptl.user_profile_option_name  upname,
           pro.profile_option_name       pvname,
           DECODE(val.level_id,
           10001, 'Site',
           10002, 'Application',
           10003, 'Responsibility',
           10004, 'User',
           10005, 'Server',
           10007, 'SERVRESP',
           'UnDef')                    lvlset,
           DECODE(to_char(val.level_id),
           '10001', ' ',
           '10002', app.application_short_name,
           '10003', rsp.responsibility_key,
           '10005', svr.node_name,
           '10006', org.name,
           '10004', usr.user_name,
           '10007', 'Serv/resp',
           'UnDef')                           vcntxt,
           TO_CHAR(val.last_update_date,'DD-MON-RR') vupdat,
           val.profile_option_value              vvalue
  FROM     fnd_profile_options           pro,
           fnd_profile_option_values     val,
           fnd_profile_options_tl ptl,
           fnd_user                      usr,
           fnd_application               app,
           fnd_responsibility            rsp,
           fnd_nodes                     svr,
           hr_operating_units            org
 WHERE     pro.profile_option_id = val.profile_option_id (+)
   AND     pro.profile_option_name = ptl.profile_option_name
   AND     ptl.language        = 'US'
   AND     upper(ptl.user_profile_option_name) like
           upper('%Sign-On:Audit Level%')
   AND     usr.user_id (+)          = val.level_value
   AND     rsp.application_id (+)   =
           val.level_value_application_id
   AND     rsp.responsibility_id (+) = val.level_value
   AND     app.application_id (+)    = val.level_value
   AND     svr.node_id (+)           = val.level_value
   AND     org.organization_id (+)   = val.level_value
 ORDER BY 1,3,4;
```

User Profile Name	Profile Name	Profile Level	Context	Last Update Date	Profile Value
Sign-On:Audit Level	SIGNONAUDI T:LEVEL	Site		16-AUG-02	D

Note: Sign-On:Audit Level **Profile-Value:** D = Form.

Oracle Application Manager (OAM) -- Database Session Monitoring/Tracing/Terminating

	System Administrator	\<Responsibility\>
	Oracle Application Manager	\<MenuSelections\>
	Dashboard	\<MenuSelections\>

Figure 11 – Oracle Application Manager – Database Session Monitoring / Tracing / Terminating

Oracle Application Manager (OAM) -- Database Session Monitoring/Tracing/Terminating

🖱 **Application Dash Board**   <MenuBar -- Top of Screen>
🖱 **Performance**   <Menu Selections>

Comment [B]: Redo this screenshot. When you do the screenshot, reformat the screen and make it narrower so that it will look bigger in the book and be easier to read

Figure 12 – Oracle Application Manager – Database Session Monitoring / Tracing / Terminating

Oracle Application Manager (OAM) -- Database Session Monitoring/Tracing/Terminating

Application Tier Hosts -or- Database Instances:
Database Sessions
🖰   **<u>91</u>**   **<Click HotSpot Database Sessions>**

Oracle Application Manager (OAM) Non-RAC
(Non Real Application Cluster)

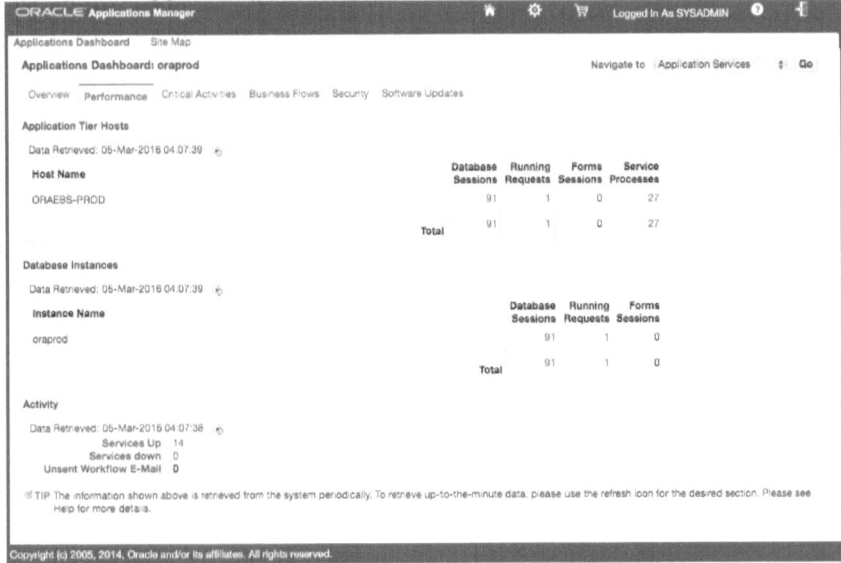

Figure 13 – Oracle Application Manager – Database Session Monitoring / Tracing / Terminating
Non-RAC (Real Application Cluster)

Oracle Application Manager (OAM) -- Database Session Monitoring/Tracing/Terminating

Application Tier Hosts -or- Database Instances:
Database Sessions

    🖱   **<u>68</u>**   **RAC-Node-1 <Click HotSpot Database Sessions>**
    🖱   **<u>115</u>** **RAC-Node-2 <Click HotSpot Database Sessions>**

Oracle Application Manager (OAM) RAC (Real Application Cluster)

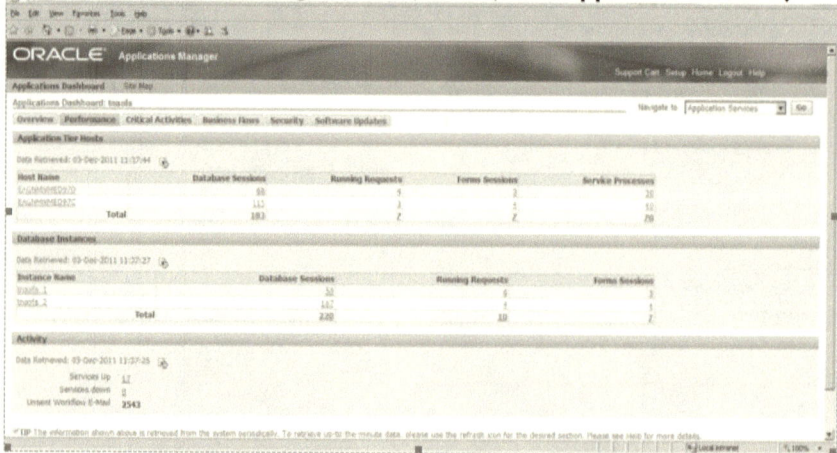

Figure 14 – Oracle Application Manager – Database Session Monitoring / Tracing / Terminating RAC (Real Application Cluster)

Oracle Application Manager (OAM) -- Database Session Monitoring/Tracing/Terminating

E-Business 11i, 12.1

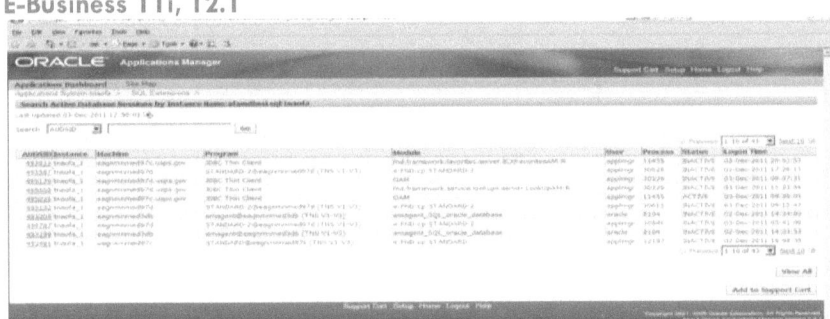

E-Business 12.2

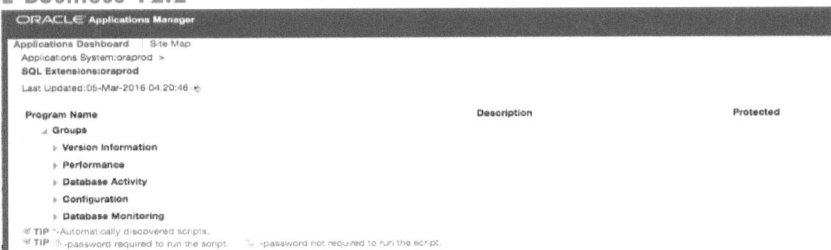

Figure 15 – Oracle Application Manager – Database Session Monitoring / Tracing / Terminating
Search Active Database Sessions by Instance Name

🖱 **View All**   <Bottom of Screen/Page>
🖱 **Sort By:**   <Click On the Column-Heading>

Report Columns:

AUDSID	Instance	Machine
Program	Module	User
Process	Status	Log-on Time

Legend:
```
RTI_PID - Runtime Instance PID <AppsTier OS Process ID>
LRs  - Session Logical Reads.
PRs  - Session Physical Reads.
CPU  - CPU used by this session, seconds.
PGA  - Session PGA memory, Kbytes.
UGA  - Session UGA memory, Kbytes.
Duration - Time elapsed since activation, hh:mm:ss.
```

Oracle Application Manager (OAM) -- Database Session Monitoring/Tracing/Terminating

E-Business 11i, 12.1

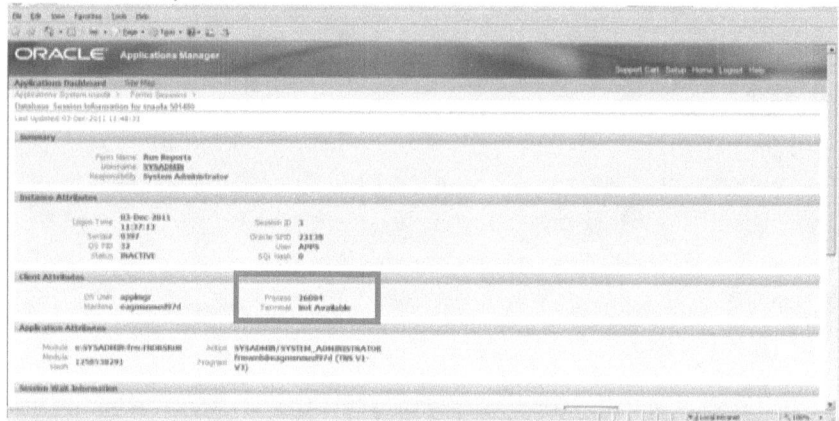

Figure 16 – Oracle Application Manager (OAM) Database Session Information – Database Session Information for a session

Summary:

Form Name: Oracle E-Business Suite Current Form-Name
Username: E-Business Suite User
Responsibility: E-Business Responsibility

Oracle Application Manager (OAM) -- Database Session Monitoring/Tracing/Terminating

E-Business 11i, 12.1

Instance Attributes: DBTier/Database

Logon Time:	Forms-Session Log-On Time
Serial:	E-Business Suite Database Session Serial#
OS PID:	Unix/Linux Operating System Process ID
Status:	E-Business Suite Database Status (ACTIVE/INACTIVE/KILLED/etc)
Session ID:	E-Business Suite Database Session ID
Oracle SPID:	E-Business Suite DBTier OS Process ID
User:	APPS
SQL Hash	E-Business Suite Database SQL-Statement (Currently Executing SQL-Statement).
Optional: DBTier:	To Manually Kill the Oracle Database Session: Unix/Linux Command: sqlplus / as sysdba ALTER SYSTEM KILL SESSION 'Session ID, Session Serial#'

Oracle Application Manager (OAM) -- Database Session Monitoring/Tracing/Terminating

E-Business 11i, 12.1

Client Attributes: DBTier/Database

OS User:	Forms-Session Log-On Time
Machine:	AppsTier Server-Name
Process:	AppsTier Unix-Process-ID
Terminal:	AppsTier Terminal-Name

AppsTier:

Unix/Linux Command: kill -15 Unix-Process-ID

Application Attributes: Form/Module

Module:	Form Name (Short Name)
Module Hash:	Module Hash
Action:	Module
Program:	Program that is executing this
SQL.	

Oracle Application Manager (OAM) -- Database Session Monitoring/Tracing/Terminating

E-Business 11i, 12.1

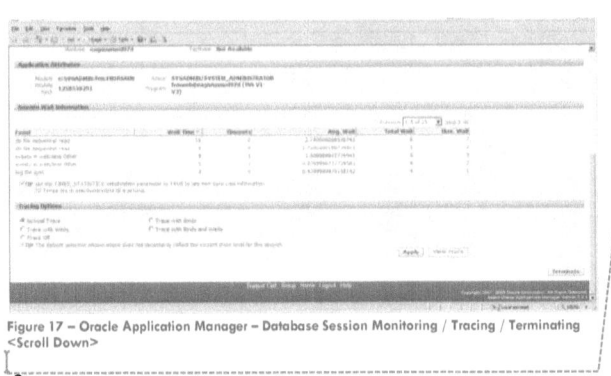

> **Comment [B]:** Redo this screenshot. When you do the screenshot, reformat the screen and make it narrower so that it will look bigger in the book and be easier to read

Figure 17 – Oracle Application Manager – Database Session Monitoring / Tracing / Terminating
<Scroll Down>

🖰   **Trace with Binds and Waits**
🖰   **Apply**

🔍 Confirmation

The trace has been turned on with binds and waits. The trace file is: /d200/oracle/rndupg/12.1.0/rdbms/log/rndupg_ora_10521.trc

-or-

🖰   **Terminate.**   **Terminate/Kill the Selected Database Session**

Oracle Application Manager (OAM) -- Database Session Monitoring/Tracing/Terminating

E-Business 11i, 12.1

Comment [B]: Redo this screenshot. When you do the screenshot, reformat screen and make it narrower so that it look bigger in the book and be easier read

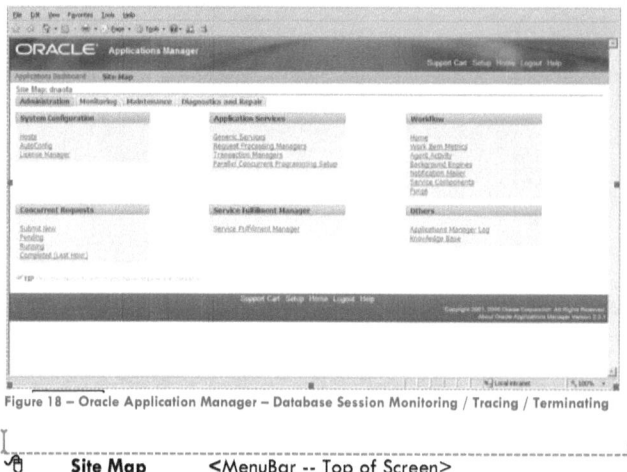

Figure 18 – Oracle Application Manager – Database Session Monitoring / Tracing / Terminating

| | **Site Map** | <MenuBar -- Top of Screen> |
| | **Monitoring** | <MenuSelections> |

Oracle Application Manager (OAM) -- Database Session Monitoring/Tracing/Terminating

E-Business 11i, 12.1

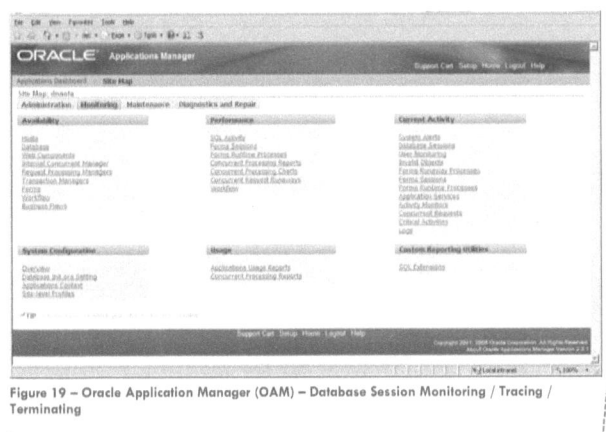

Figure 19 – Oracle Application Manager (OAM) – Database Session Monitoring / Tracing / Terminating

Comment [B]: Redo this screenshot. When you do the screenshot, reformat the screen and make it narrower so that it will look bigger in the book and be easier to read

Performance   Middle of the Screen
SQL Activity

Oracle Application Manager (OAM) -- Database Session Monitoring/Tracing/Terminating

E-Business 11i, 12.1

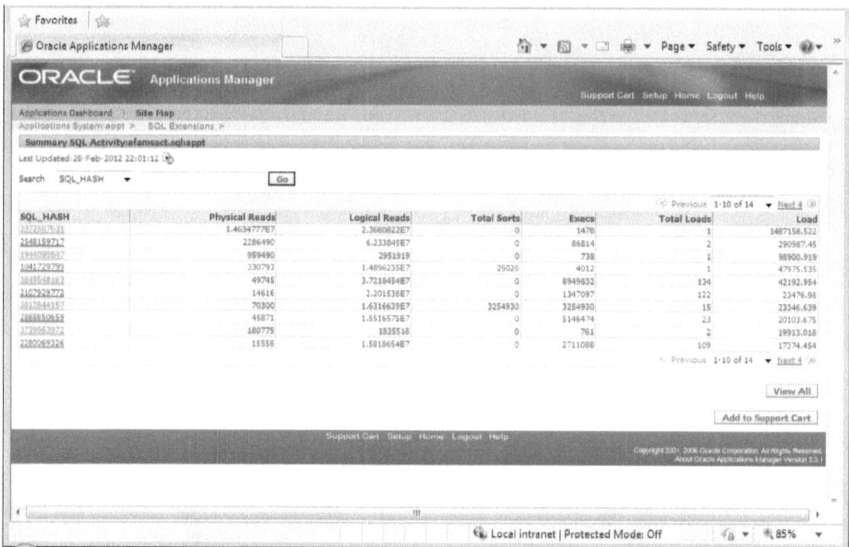

Figure 20 – Oracle Application Manager (OAM) – Session Monitoring / Tracing / Terminating

🖑 **SQL_HASH**	Middle of the Screen
🖑 **SQL_HASH ID**	

Oracle Application Manager (OAM) -- Database Session Monitoring/Tracing/Terminating

E-Business 11i, 12.1

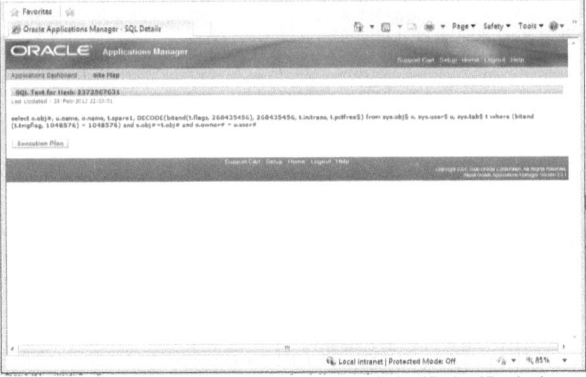

Figure 21 – Oracle Application Manager (OAM) – Session Monitoring / Tracing / Terminating – This screen shows the SQL Text for the Hash. Click on the Execution Plan button to see the plan.

This is the SQL-Statement that is currently executing in this Database Session.

Oracle Application Manager (OAM) -- Database Session Monitoring/Tracing/Terminating

E-Business 11i, 12.1

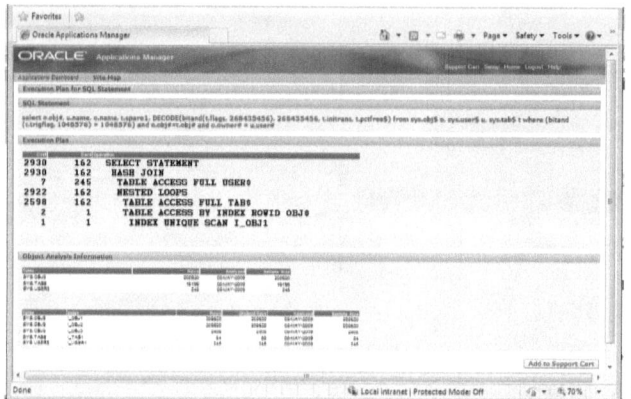

Figure 22 – Oracle Application Manager – Session Monitoring / Tracing / Terminating – This screen shows the Execution Plan and the Object Analysis Information.

These are the Database details for the SQL-Statement that is currently executing in this Database Session.

Oracle Application Manager (OAM) -- Database Session Monitoring/Tracing/Terminating

E-Business 12.2

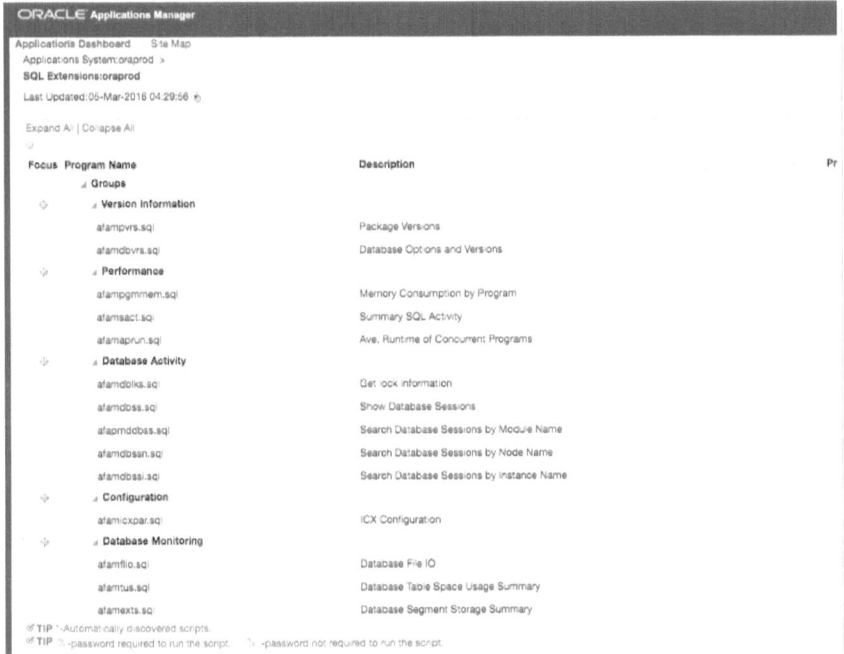

Select from the following Available Database Session Details:

Version Information	Performance	Database Activity
Configuration	Database Monitoring	

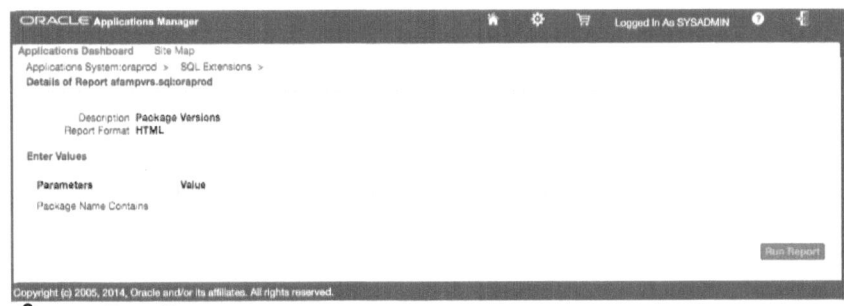

🖱   **Run Report**

CHAPTER 4
E-BUSINESS SUITE 11I TO 12.2.5 -- OAM PERFORMANCE MONITORING – FORMS SESSIONS

OAM: Oracle Application Manager is an Oracle E-Business Suite Seeded Responsibility. The Oracle Application Manager Seeded Performance Monitoring Screens can be used to monitor, trace and terminate Oracle E-Business Suite Forms Sessions.

Special Note:

- Since the E-Business Suite ICX (Internet Connections) are recorded in the ICX Tables, you can examine the ICX Connections that are current and/or historical. Additionally, the ICX history is available until the Concurrent Request: *Purge Inactive Sessions* is executed and the ICX activity is purged.

- The Forms-Connections, on the other hand, are only available when they are active. So, when a Forms User disconnects, the form information will no longer show a User with an open Forms Session.

- **Profile Options**
  Sign-On:Audit Level **must be set to** 'FORM' **at the** SITE **level.**

  SQL-Query to identify the E-Business Suite SignOn Audit Level appears on the next page.

Special Note: (Continued)

```
SELECT      ptl.user_profile_option_name   upname,
            pro.profile_option_name        pvname,
            DECODE(val.level_id,
            10001, 'Site',
            10002, 'Application',
            10003, 'Responsibility',
            10004, 'User',
            10005, 'Server',
            10007, 'SERVRESP',
            'UnDef')                   lvlset,
            DECODE(to_char(val.level_id),
            '10001', ' ',
            '10002', app.application_short_name,
            '10003', rsp.responsibility_key,
            '10005', svr.node_name,
            '10006', org.name,
            '10004', usr.user_name,
            '10007', 'Serv/resp',
             'UnDef')                           vcntxt,
            TO_CHAR(val.last_update_date,'DD-MON-RR') vupdat,
            val.profile_option_value              vvalue
    FROM    fnd_profile_options            pro,
            fnd_profile_option_values      val,
            fnd_profile_options_tl ptl,
            fnd_user                       usr,
            fnd_application                app,
            fnd_responsibility             rsp,
            fnd_nodes                      svr,
            hr_operating_units             org
   WHERE    pro.profile_option_id = val.profile_option_id (+)
     AND    pro.profile_option_name = ptl.profile_option_name
     AND    ptl.language          = 'US'
     AND    upper(ptl.user_profile_option_name) like
            upper('%Sign-On:Audit Level%')
     AND     usr.user_id (+)          = val.level_value
     AND     rsp.application_id (+)   =
              val.level_value_application_id
     AND     rsp.responsibility_id (+) = val.level_value
     AND     app.application_id (+)   = val.level_value
     AND     svr.node_id (+)         = val.level_value
     AND     org.organization_id (+)  = val.level_value
   ORDER BY 1,3,4;
```

User Profile Name	Profile Name	Profile Level	Context	Last Update Date	Profile Value
Sign-On:Audit Level	SIGNONAUDI T:LEVEL	Site		16-AUG-02	D

Note: Sign-On:Audit Level **Profile-Value:** D = Form.

Oracle Application Manager (OAM) -- Forms Session Monitoring/Tracing/Terminating

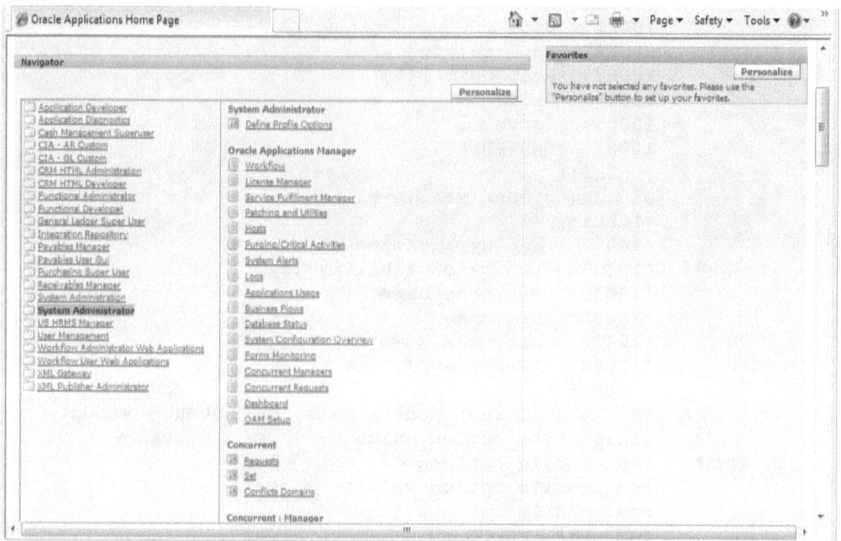

Figure 23 – Oracle Application Manager (OAM) – Forms Monitoring / Tracing / Terminating.

✍	**System Administrator**	\<Responsibility\>
✍	**Oracle Application Manager**	\<MenuSelections\>
✍	**Dashboard**	\<MenuSelections\>

Oracle Application Manager (OAM) -- Forms Session Monitoring/Tracing/Terminating

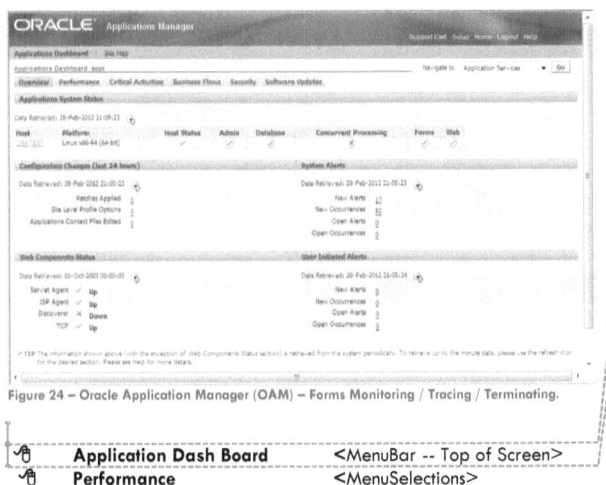

Figure 24 – Oracle Application Manager (OAM) – Forms Monitoring / Tracing / Terminating.

🖱 **Application Dash Board**   <MenuBar -- Top of Screen>
🖱 **Performance**   <MenuSelections>

Application Tier Hosts -or- Database Instances:
Forms Sessions
    🖱   **3**   <Click On The Number of Forms Sessions>

Comment [B]: Redo this screenshot. When you do the screenshot, reformat the screen and make it narrower so that it will look bigger in the book and be easier to read

Comment [B]: Redo this screenshot. When you do the screenshot, reformat the screen and make it narrower so that it will look bigger in the book and be easier to read

Oracle Application Manager (OAM) — Forms Session Monitoring/Tracing/Terminating

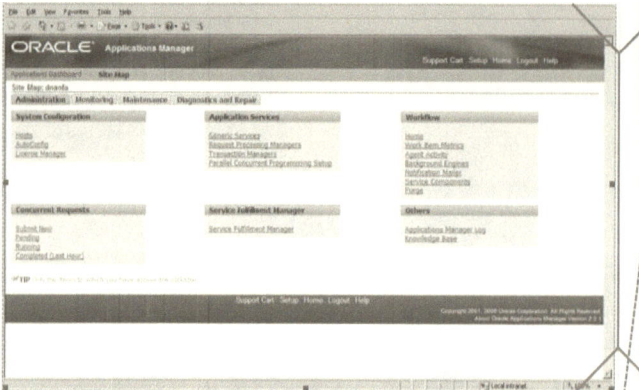

Figure 25 – Oracle Application Manager (OAM) – Forms Monitoring / Tracing / Terminating.

🖰	**Site Map**	<MenuBar -- Top of Screen>
🖰	**Monitoring**	<MenuSelections>

Oracle Application Manager (OAM) — Forms Session Monitoring/Tracing/Terminating

> **Comment [B]:** Redo this screenshot. When you do the screenshot, reformat the screen and make it narrower so that it will look bigger in the book and be easier to read

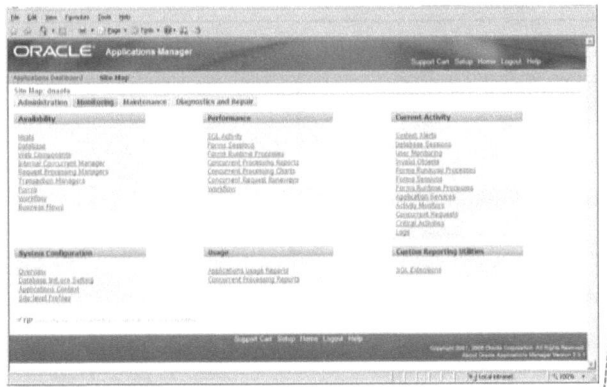

Figure 26 – Oracle Application Manager (OAM) – Forms Monitoring / Tracing / Terminating.

Performance   Middle of Screen
Form Sessions

Oracle Application Manager (OAM) -- Forms Session Monitoring/Tracing/Terminating

> **Comment [B]:** Redo this screenshot. When you do the screenshot, reforma screen and make it narrower so that it look bigger in the book and be easier read

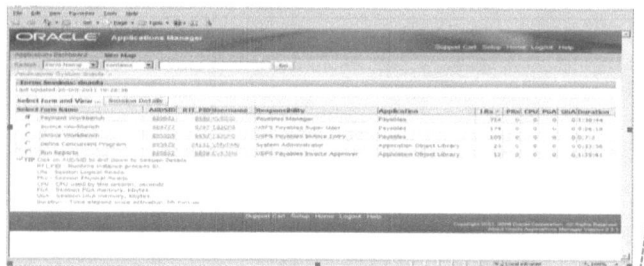

Figure 27 – Oracle Application Manager (OAM) – Forms Monitoring / Tracing / Terminating.

🖱 **AUDSID**   Select User to be Monitored/Traced/Terminated

🖱 **View All**   <Bottom of Screen/Page>
🖱 **Sort By:**   <Click On the Column-Heading>

Report Columns:

AUDSID	Instance	Machine
Program	Module	User
Process	Status	Log-on Time

Legend:
```
RTI_PID - Runtime Instance PID <AppsTier OS Process ID)
LRs - Session Logical Reads.
PRs - Session Physical Reads.
CPU - CPU used by this session, seconds.
PGA - Session PGA memory, Kbytes.
UGA - Session UGA memory, Kbytes.
Duration - Time elapsed since activation, hh:mm:ss.
```

Oracle Application Manager (OAM) -- Forms Session Monitoring/Tracing/Terminating

Comment [B]: Redo this screenshot. When you do the screenshot, reformat the screen and make it narrower so that it will look bigger in the book and be easier to read

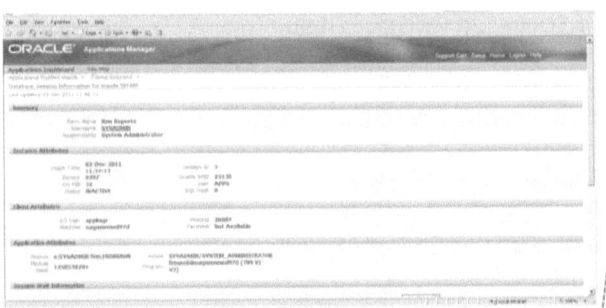

Figure 28 – Oracle Application Manager (OAM) – Forms Monitoring / Tracing / Terminating.

Summary:
======

Form Name:	Oracle E-Business Suite Current Form-Name
Username:	E-Business Suite User
Responsibility:	E-Business Responsibility

Oracle Application Manager (OAM) -- Forms Session Monitoring/Tracing/Terminating

Instance Attributes: DBTier/Database

Logon Time:	Forms-Session Log-On Time
Serial:	E-Business Suite Database Session Serial#
OS PID:	Unix/Linux Operating System Process ID
Status:	E-Business Suite Database Status (ACTIVE/INACTIVE/KILLED/etc)
Session ID:	E-Business Suite Database Session ID
Oracle SPID:	E-Business Suite DBTier OS Process ID
User:	APPS
SQL Hash	E-Business Suite Database SQL-Statement (Currently Executing SQL-Statement).
Optional: DBTier:	To Manually Kill the Oracle Database Session: Unix/Linux Command: sqlplus / as sysdba ALTER SYSTEM KILL SESSION 'Session ID, Session Serial#'

Oracle Application Manager (OAM) -- Forms Session Monitoring/Tracing/Terminating

Client Attributes: DBTier/Database

OS User:	Forms-Session Log-On Time
Machine:	AppsTier Server-Name
Process:	AppsTier Unix-Process-ID
Terminal:	AppsTier Terminal-Name

AppsTier:
Unix/Linux Command: kill -15 Unix-Process-ID

Application Attributes: Form/Module

Module:	Form Name (Short Name)
Module Hash:	Module Hash
Action:	Module
Program:	Program that is executing this SQL.

Oracle Application Manager (OAM) -- Forms Session Monitoring/Tracing/Terminating

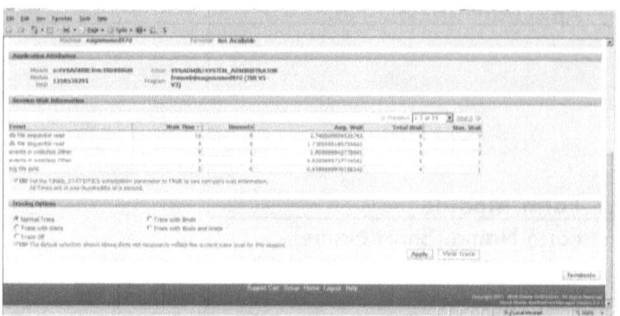

Figure 29 – Oracle Application Manager (OAM) – Forms Monitoring / Tracing / Terminating.

🖱 **Trace with Binds and Waits**
🖱 **Apply**
-or-
🖱 **Terminate.**   **Terminate/Kill the Selected Forms Session.**

CHAPTER 5
E-BUSINESS SUITE 11I TO 12.2.5 -- OAM PERFORMANCE MONITORING – CONCURRENT REQUESTS

OAM: Oracle Application Manager is an Oracle E-Business Suite Seeded Responsibility. The Oracle Application Manager Seeded Performance Monitoring Screens can be used to monitor, trace and terminate Oracle E-Business Suite Concurrent-Processing Sessions.

Special Note:

- Since the E-Business Suite ICX (Internet Connections) are recorded in the ICX Tables, you can examine the ICX Connections that are current and/or historical. Additionally, the ICX history is available until the Concurrent Request: *Purge Inactive Sessions* is executed and the ICX activity is purged.

- The Forms-Connections, on the other hand, are only available when they are active. So, when a Forms User disconnects, the form information will no longer show a User with an open Forms Session.

- **Profile Options**
  Sign-On:Audit Level **must be set to** 'FORM' **at the** SITE **level.**

  SQL-Query to identify the E-Business Suite SignOn Audit Level appears on the next page.

Special Note: (Continued)

```
SELECT     ptl.user_profile_option_name   upname,
           pro.profile_option_name        pvname,
           DECODE(val.level_id,
           10001, 'Site',
           10002, 'Application',
           10003, 'Responsibility',
           10004, 'User',
           10005, 'Server',
           10007, 'SERVRESP',
           'UnDef')                        lvlset,
           DECODE(to_char(val.level_id),
           '10001', '',
           '10002', app.application_short_name,
           '10003', rsp.responsibility_key,
           '10005', svr.node_name,
           '10006', org.name,
           '10004', usr.user_name,
           '10007', 'Serv/resp',
           'UnDef')                        vcntxt,
           TO_CHAR(val.last_update_date,'DD-MON-RR') vupdat,
           val.profile_option_value        vvalue
FROM       fnd_profile_options             pro,
           fnd_profile_option_values       val,
           fnd_profile_options_tl ptl,
           fnd_user                        usr,
           fnd_application                 app,
           fnd_responsibility              rsp,
           fnd_nodes                       svr,
           hr_operating_units              org
WHERE      pro.profile_option_id = val.profile_option_id (+)
  AND      pro.profile_option_name = ptl.profile_option_name
  AND      ptl.language            = 'US'
  AND      upper(ptl.user_profile_option_name) like
           upper('%Sign-On:Audit Level%')
  AND       usr.user_id (+)         = val.level_value
  AND       rsp.application_id (+)  =
            val.level_value_application_id
  AND       rsp.responsibility_id (+) = val.level_value
  AND       app.application_id (+)  = val.level_value
  AND       svr.node_id (+)         = val.level_value
  AND       org.organization_id (+) = val.level_value
ORDER BY 1,3,4;
```

User Profile Name	Profile Name	Profile Level	Context	Last Update Date	Profile Value
Sign-On:Audit Level	SIGNONAUDI T:LEVEL	Site		16-AUG-02	D

Note: Sign-On:Audit Level Profile-Value: D = Form.

Oracle Application Manager (OAM) -- Concurrent Processing Session Monitoring/Tracing/Terminating

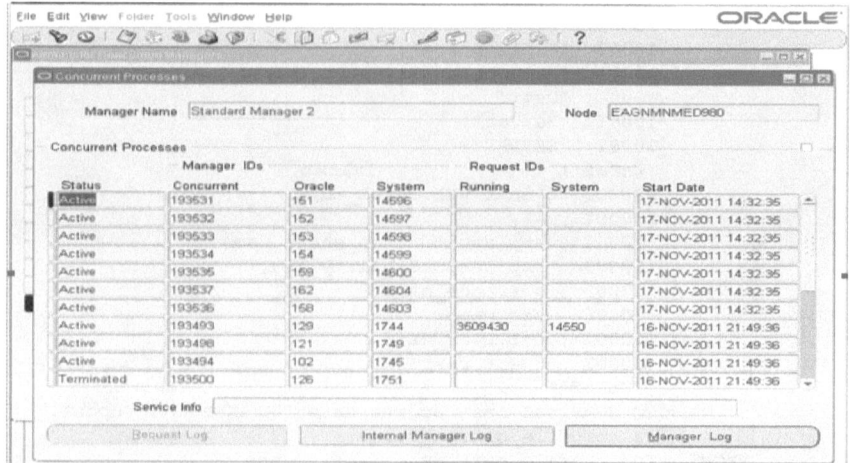

Figure 30 – Oracle Application Manager (OAM) – ConcRequest Monitoring / Tracing / Terminating

    🖱️   **System Administrator**   <Responsibility>
    🖱️   **Concurrent Manager**   <MenuSelections>
    🖱️   **Administrator**   <MenuSelections>
    🖱️   **Processes**   <MenuSelections>

Oracle Application Manager (OAM) -- Concurrent Processing Session Monitoring/Tracing/Terminating

Note: There is ONLY one (1) Active Concurrent-Request: Request-ID "System" ID: 14550

APPSTier: Unix/Linux: ps -efa | grep 14550

```
applmgr  14550  1744  0 14:32 ?         00:00:02
/u00shared/apps/10.1.2/bin/rwrun
mode=character P_CONC_REQUEST_ID=3509430 p_from_date='2014/06/01
00:00:00' p_to_date='
00:00:00' p_include_feeder='Y' p_incl_etrv='Y' p_sample_size='100'
report=/a00shared/ap/reports/US/XXAPAUDIT.rdf userid=APPS batch=yes
destype=file
desname=/a00shared/APPLCSF/out/o3509430.outdesformat=/u00shared/app
s/appl/fnd/12.0.0/
reports/HPW pagesize=180x66
```

Oracle Application Manager (OAM) -- Concurrent Processing Session Monitoring/Tracing/Terminating

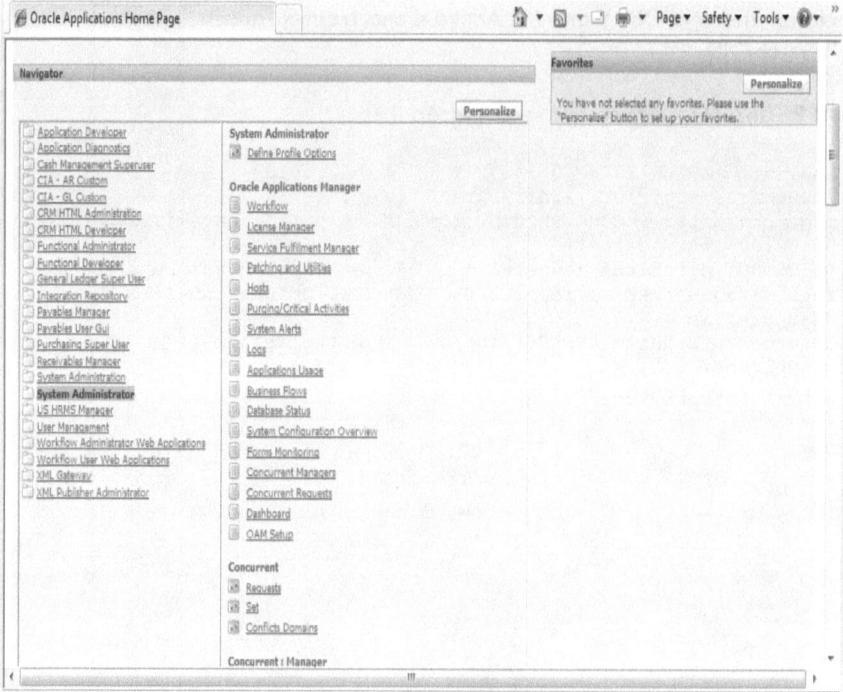

Figure 31 – Oracle Application Manager (OAM) – ConcRequest Monitoring / Tracing / Terminating

🖱 **System Administrator**　　　　　<Responsibility>
🖱 **Oracle Application Manager**　<MenuSelections>

Oracle Application Manager (OAM) -- Concurrent Processing Session Monitoring/Tracing/Terminating

> **Comment [B]:** Redo this screenshot. When you do the screenshot, reformat the screen and make it narrower so that it will look bigger in the book and be easier to read

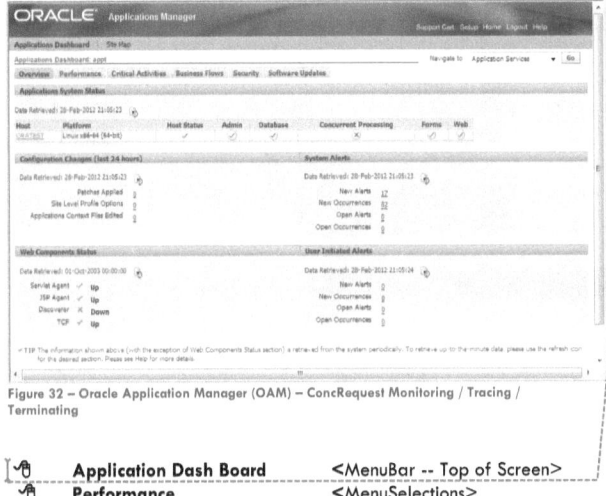

Figure 32 – Oracle Application Manager (OAM) – ConcRequest Monitoring / Tracing / Terminating

🖱 **Application Dash Board**   \<MenuBar -- Top of Screen>
🖱 **Performance**   \<MenuSelections>

Application Tier Hosts -or- Database Instances:
Concurrent Processing Sessions
    🖱   <u>3</u>   \<Click On The Number of Concurrent Sessions>

Oracle Application Manager (OAM) -- Concurrent Processing Session Monitoring/Tracing/Terminating

Comment [B]: Redo this screenshot. When you do the screenshot, reforma screen and make it narrower so that it look bigger in the book and be easier read

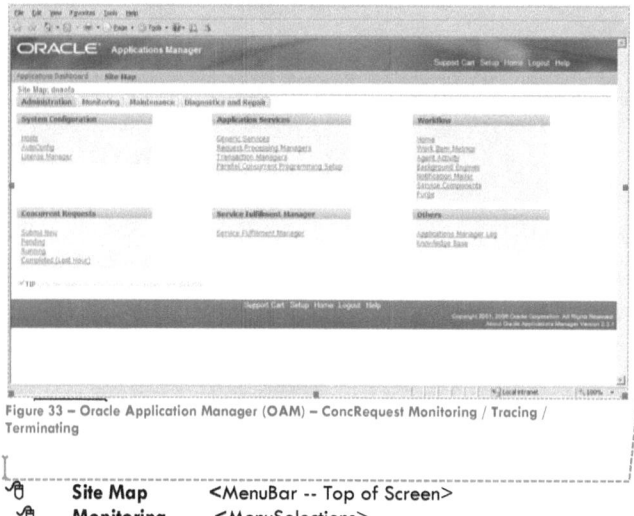

Figure 33 – Oracle Application Manager (OAM) – ConcRequest Monitoring / Tracing / Terminating

🖰 **Site Map**   <MenuBar -- Top of Screen>
🖰 **Monitoring**   <MenuSelections>

Oracle Application Manager (OAM) -- Concurrent Processing Session Monitoring/Tracing/Terminating

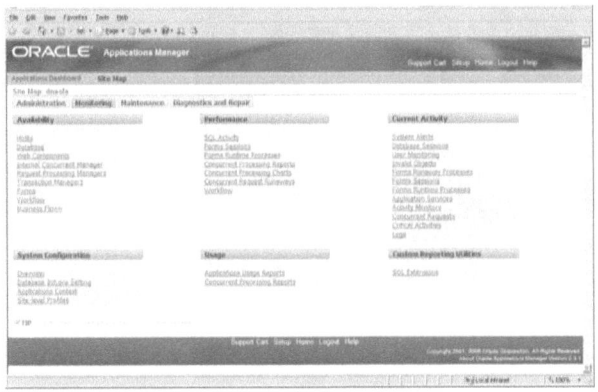

Figure 35 – Oracle Application Manager (OAM) – ConcRequest Monitoring / Tracing / Terminating

Performance   <MenuBar -- Top of Screen>
Concurrent Processing Reports <Menu Selections>

CHAPTER 6
E-BUSINESS SUITE 12.2 PERFORMANCE MONITORING

OAM: Oracle Application Manager is an Oracle E-Business Suite seeded Responsibility. The Oracle Application Manager seeded Performance Monitoring Screens can be used to monitor, trace and terminate:

> Oracle E-Business Suite Database Sessions
> Oracle E-Business Suite Forms Sessions
> Oracle E-Business Suite Concurrent Processing Sessions.

Special Note:

- Since the E-Business Suite ICX (Internet Connections) are recorded in the ICX Tables, you can examine the ICX Connections that are current and/or historical. Additionally, the ICX history is available until the Concurrent Request: *Purge Inactive Sessions* is executed and the ICX activity is purged.

- The Forms-Connections, on the other hand, are only available when they are active. So, when a Forms User disconnects, the form information will no longer show a User with an open Forms Session.

- **Profile Options**
  Sign-On:Audit Level must be set to 'FORM' at the SITE level.

  SQL-Query to identify the E-Business Suite SignOn Audit Level appears on the next page.

Special Note: (Continued)

```
SELECT      ptl.user_profile_option_name  upname,
            pro.profile_option_name        pvname,
            DECODE(val.level_id,
            10001, 'Site',
            10002, 'Application',
            10003, 'Responsibility',
            10004, 'User',
            10005, 'Server',
            10007, 'SERVRESP',
            'UnDef')                    lvlset,
            DECODE(to_char(val.level_id),
            '10001', '',
            '10002', app.application_short_name,
            '10003', rsp.responsibility_key,
            '10005', svr.node_name,
            '10006', org.name,
            '10004', usr.user_name,
            '10007', 'Serv/resp',
             'UnDef')                          vcntxt,
            TO_CHAR(val.last_update_date,'DD-MON-RR') vupdat,
            val.profile_option_value                  vvalue
    FROM    fnd_profile_options             pro,
            fnd_profile_option_values       val,
            fnd_profile_options_tl ptl,
            fnd_user                        usr,
            fnd_application                 app,
            fnd_responsibility              rsp,
            fnd_nodes                       svr,
            hr_operating_units              org
   WHERE    pro.profile_option_id = val.profile_option_id (+)
     AND    pro.profile_option_name = ptl.profile_option_name
     AND    ptl.language          = 'US'
     AND    upper(ptl.user_profile_option_name) like
            upper('%Sign-On:Audit Level%')
     AND    usr.user_id (+)            = val.level_value
     AND    rsp.application_id (+)   =
             val.level_value_application_id
     AND    rsp.responsibility_id (+) = val.level_value
     AND    app.application_id (+)   = val.level_value
     AND    svr.node_id (+)          = val.level_value
     AND    org.organization_id (+)  = val.level_value
   ORDER BY 1,3,4;
```

User Profile Name	Profile Name	Profile Level	Context	Last Update Date	Profile Value
Sign-On:Audit Level	SIGNONAUDI T:LEVEL	Site		16-AUG-02	D

Note: Sign-On:Audit Level **Profile-Value: D = Form.**

CHAPTER 7
E-BUSINESS SUITE 12.2 -- OAM
PERFORMANCE MONITORING – DATABASE
SESSIONS

OAM: Oracle Application Manager is an Oracle E-Business Suite seeded Responsibility. The Oracle Application Manager Seeded Performance Monitoring Screens can be used to monitor, trace and terminate Oracle E-Business Suite Database Sessions.

Special Note:

- Since the E-Business Suite ICX (Internet Connections) are recorded in the ICX Tables, you can examine the ICX Connections that are current and/or historical. Additionally, the ICX history is available until the Concurrent Request: ***Purge Inactive Sessions*** is executed and the ICX activity is purged.

- The Forms-Connections, on the other hand, are only available when they are active. So, when a Forms User disconnects, the form information will no longer show a User with an open Forms Session.

- **Profile Options**
  Sign-On:Audit Level **must be set to** 'FORM' **at the** SITE **level.**

  SQL-Query to identify the E-Business Suite SignOn Audit Level appears on the next page.

Special Note: (Continued)

```
SELECT      ptl.user_profile_option_name  upname,
            pro.profile_option_name        pvname,
            DECODE(val.level_id,
            10001, 'Site',
            10002, 'Application',
            10003, 'Responsibility',
            10004, 'User',
            10005, 'Server',
            10007, 'SERVRESP',
            'UnDef')                        lvlset,
            DECODE(to_char(val.level_id),
            '10001', ' ',
            '10002', app.application_short_name,
            '10003', rsp.responsibility_key,
            '10005', svr.node_name,
            '10006', org.name,
            '10004', usr.user_name,
            '10007', 'Serv/resp',
            'UnDef')                                vcntxt,
            TO_CHAR(val.last_update_date,'DD-MON-RR') vupdat,
            val.profile_option_value                vvalue
FROM        fnd_profile_options            pro,
            fnd_profile_option_values      val,
            fnd_profile_options_tl ptl,
            fnd_user                       usr,
            fnd_application                app,
            fnd_responsibility             rsp,
            fnd_nodes                      svr,
            hr_operating_units             org
WHERE       pro.profile_option_id = val.profile_option_id (+)
   AND      pro.profile_option_name = ptl.profile_option_name
   AND      ptl.language          = 'US'
   AND      upper(ptl.user_profile_option_name) like
            upper('%Sign-On:Audit Level%')
   AND       usr.user_id (+)          = val.level_value
   AND       rsp.application_id (+)   =
             val.level_value_application_id
   AND       rsp.responsibility_id (+) = val.level_value
   AND       app.application_id (+)   = val.level_value
   AND       svr.node_id (+)          = val.level_value
   AND       org.organization_id (+)  = val.level_value
ORDER BY 1,3,4;
```

```
User                                       Last
Profile          Profile    Profile        Update     Profile
Name             Name       Level   Context Date       Value
---------------  ---------- --------- ---------- --------- -------
Sign-On:Audit    SIGNONAUDI Site             16-AUG-02 D
Level            T:LEVEL
```

Note: Sign-On:Audit Level **Profile-Value: D = Form.**

Oracle Application Manager (OAM) -- Database Session Monitoring/Tracing/Terminating

Figure 11 – Oracle Application Manager (OAM) – Database Session Monitoring / Tracing / Terminating.

	**System Administrator**	<Responsibility>
	Oracle Application Manager	<MenuSelections>
	Dashboard	<MenuSelections>

Oracle Application Manager (OAM) — Database Session Monitoring/Tracing/Terminating

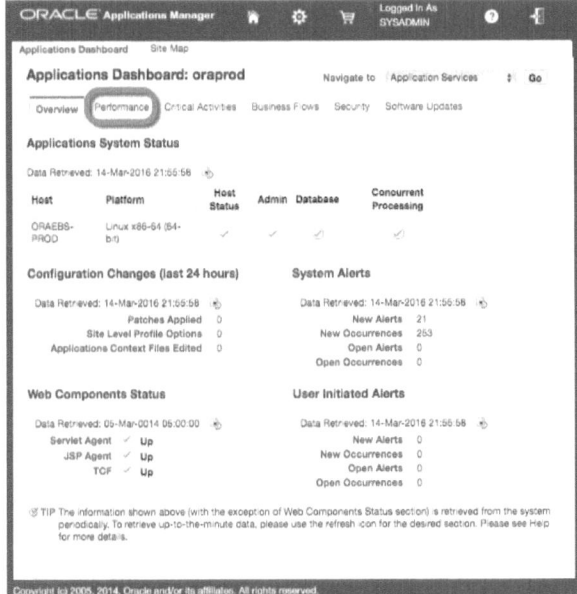

Figure 35 – Oracle Application Manager (OAM) – Database Session Monitoring / Tracing / Terminating

| | **Application Dash Board** | <MenuBar -- Top of Screen> |
| | **Performance** | <Menu Selections> |

Oracle Application Manager (OAM) -- Database Session Monitoring/Tracing/Terminating

Comment [B]: Redo this screenshot. When you do the screenshot, reformat screen and make it narrower so that it look bigger in the book and be easier read.

Oracle Application Manager (OAM) Non-RAC (Real Application Cluster)

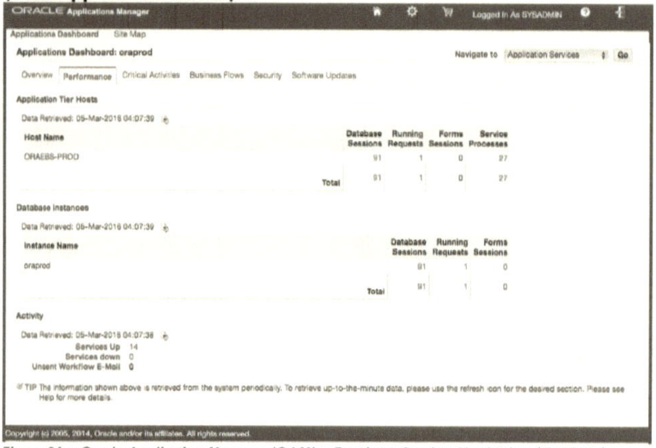

Figure 36 – Oracle Application Manager (OAM) – Database Session Monitoring / Tracing / Terminating - Non-RAC (Real Application Cluster)

Application Tier Hosts -or- Database Instances: Database Sessions

91 <Click HotSpot Database Sessions>

Oracle Application Manager (OAM) -- Database Session Monitoring/Tracing/Terminating

Oracle Application Manager (OAM) RAC (Real Application Cluster)

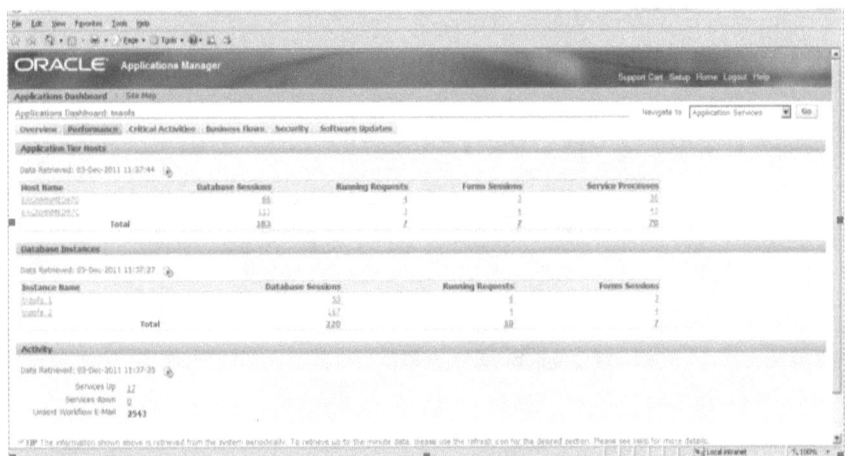

Figure 37 – Oracle Application Manager (OAM) – Database Session Monitoring / Tracing / Terminating – RAC (Real Application Cluster)

Application Tier Hosts -or- Database Instances:
Database Sessions

     68   RAC-Node-1 <Click HotSpot Database Sessions>

     115 RAC-Node-2 <Click HotSpot Database Sessions>

Oracle Application Manager (OAM) -- Database Session Monitoring/Tracing/Terminating

E-Business 11i, 12.1

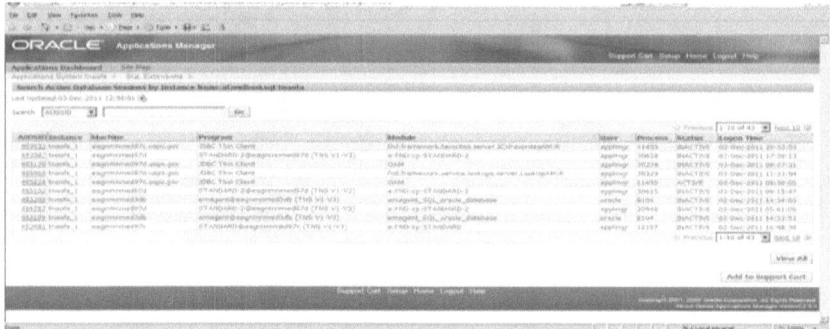

E-Business 12.2

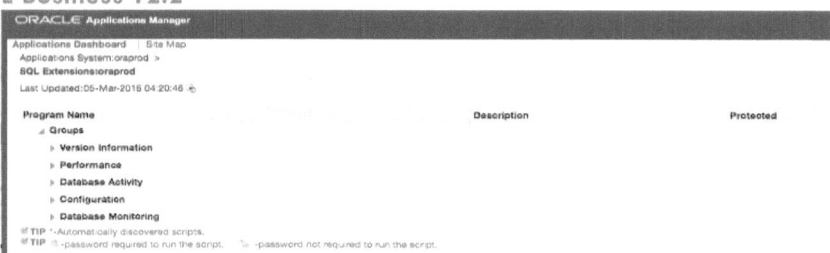

Figure 38 – Oracle Application Manager (OAM) – Database Session Monitoring / Tracing / Terminating – Search Active Database Sessions by Instance Name

 **View All**   \<Bottom of Screen/Page\>
 **Sort By:**   \<Click On the Column-Heading\>

Report Columns:

AUDSID	Instance	Machine
Program	Module	User
Process	Status	Log-onTime

Legend:

```
RTI_PID - Runtime Instance PID <AppsTier OS Process ID)
LRs - Session Logical Reads.
PRs - Session Physical Reads.
CPU - CPU used by this session, seconds.
PGA - Session PGA memory, Kbytes.
UGA - Session UGA memory, Kbytes.
Duration - Time elapsed since activation, hh:mm:ss.
```

Oracle Application Manager (OAM) — Database Session Monitoring/Tracing/Terminating

Comment [B]: Redo this screenshot. When you do the screenshot, reformat the screen and make it narrower so that it will look bigger in the book and be easier to read

E-Business 11i, 12.1

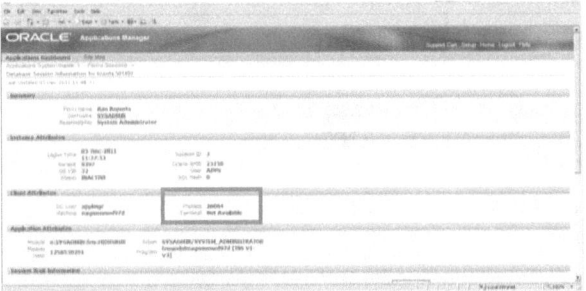

Figure 39 – Oracle Application Manager (OAM) Database Session Information – Database session Information for a session

Summary:

Form Name:	Oracle E-Business Suite Current Form-Name
Username:	E-Business Suite User
Responsibility:	E-Business Responsibility

Oracle Application Manager (OAM) -- Database Session Monitoring/Tracing/Terminating

E-Business 11i, 12.1

Instance Attributes: DBTier/Database

Logon Time: Forms-Session Log-On Time

Serial: E-Business Suite Database Session Serial#

OS PID: Unix/Linux Operating System Process ID

Status: E-Business Suite Database Status
                   (ACTIVE/INACTIVE/KILLED/etc)

Session ID: E-Business Suite Database Session ID

Oracle SPID: E-Business Suite DBTier OS Process ID

User: APPS

SQL Hash   E-Business Suite Database SQL-Statement
                   (Currently Executing SQL-Statement).

Optional: To Manually Kill the Oracle Database Session:
DBTier: Unix/Linux Command:
                   sqlplus / as sysdba
                   ALTER SYSTEM KILL SESSION 'Session ID, Session Serial#'

Oracle Application Manager (OAM) -- Database Session Monitoring/Tracing/Terminating

E-Business 11i, 12.1

Client Attributes: DBTier/Database

OS User:	Forms-Session Log-On Time
Machine:	AppsTier Server-Name
Process:	AppsTier Unix-Process-ID
Terminal:	AppsTier Terminal-Name

AppsTier:
Unix/Linux Command: kill -15 Unix-Process-ID

Application Attributes: Form/Module

Module:	Form Name (Short Name)
Module Hash:	Module Hash
Action:	Module
Program:	Program that is executing this
SQL.	

Oracle Application Manager (OAM) -- Database Session Monitoring/Tracing/Terminating

E-Business 11i, 12.1

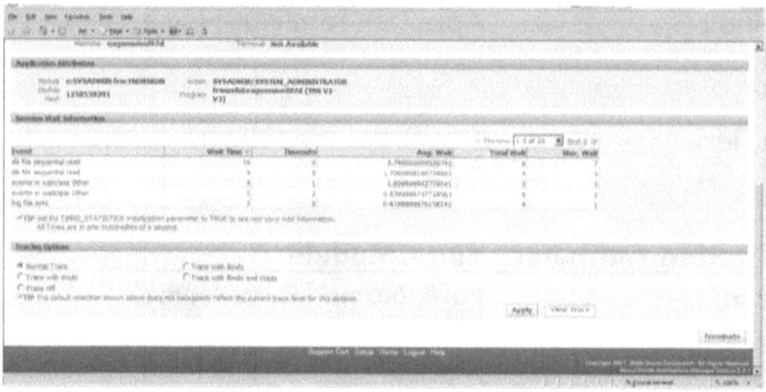

Figure 40 – Oracle Application Manager (OAM) – Database Session Monitoring / Tracing / Terminating <Scroll Down>

🖰 **Trace with Binds and Waits**

🖰 **Apply**

-or-

🖰 **Terminate.**   **Terminate/Kill the Selected Database Session**

Oracle Application Manager (OAM) -- Database Session Monitoring/Tracing/Terminating

E-Business 11i, 12.1

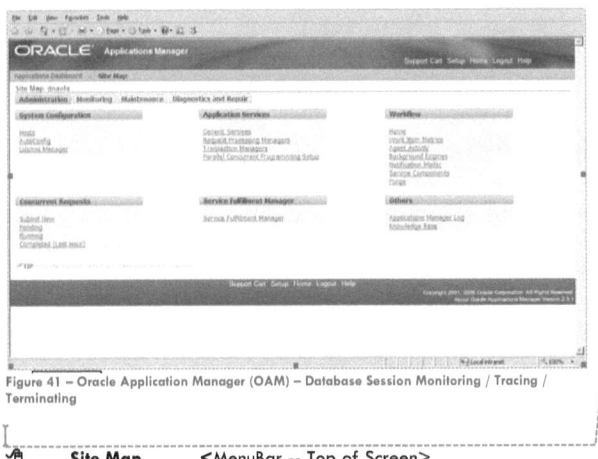

Figure 41 – Oracle Application Manager (OAM) – Database Session Monitoring / Tracing / Terminating

> **Comment [B]:** Redo this screenshot. When you do the screenshot, reformat the screen and make it narrower so that it will look bigger in the book and be easier to read

Site Map   \<MenuBar -- Top of Screen\>
Monitoring   \<MenuSelections\>

Oracle Application Manager (OAM) -- Database Session Monitoring/Tracing/Terminating

E-Business 11i, 12.1

Comment [B]: Redo this screenshot. When you do the screenshot, reforma screen and make it narrower so that it look bigger in the book and be easier read

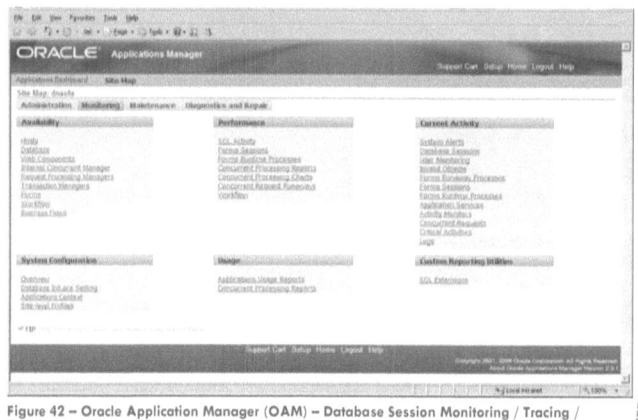

Figure 42 – Oracle Application Manager (OAM) – Database Session Monitoring / Tracing / Terminating

Performance	Middle of the Screen
SQL Activity	

Oracle Application Manager (OAM) -- Database Session Monitoring/Tracing/Terminating

E-Business 11i, 12.1

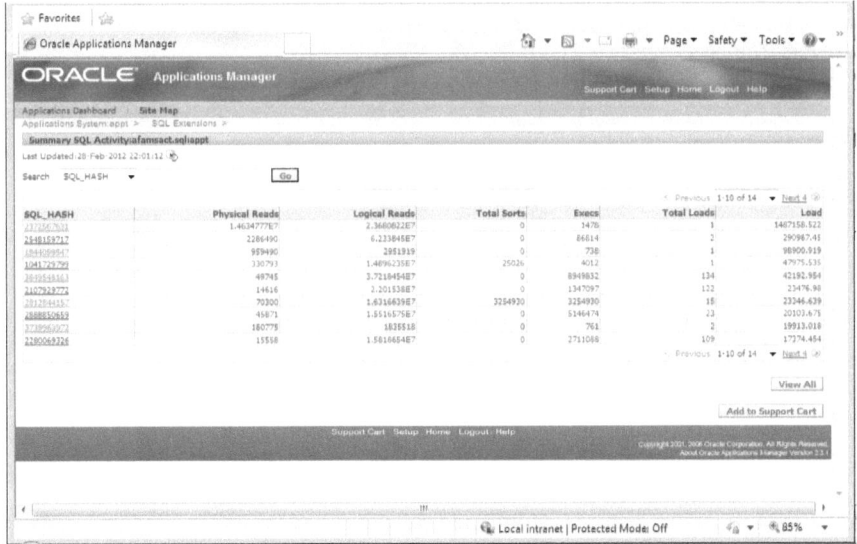

Figure 43 – Oracle Application Manager (OAM) – Session Monitoring / Tracing / Terminating

🖑   **SQL_HASH**   Middle of the Screen

🖑   **SQL_HASH ID**

Oracle Application Manager (OAM) -- Database Session Monitoring/Tracing/Terminating

E-Business 11i, 12.1

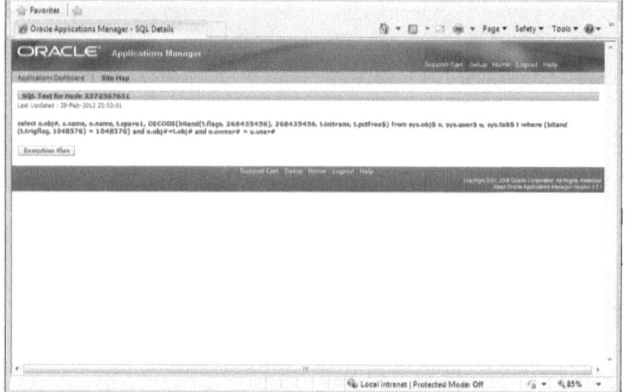

Figure 44 – Oracle Application Manager (OAM) – Session Monitoring / Tracing / Terminating – This screen shows the SQL Text for the Hash. Click on the Execution Plan button to see the plan.

This is the SQL-Statement that is currently executing in this Database Session.

Oracle Application Manager (OAM) -- Database Session Monitoring/Tracing/Terminating

E-Business 11i, 12.1

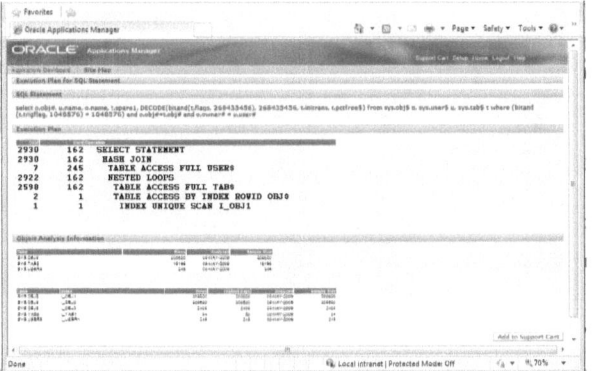

Figure 45 – Oracle Application Manager (OAM) – Session Monitoring / Tracing / Terminating – This screen shows the Execution Plan and the Object Analysis Information.

These are the Database details for the SQL-Statement that is currently executing in this Database Session.

Oracle Application Manager (OAM) -- Database Session Monitoring/Tracing/Terminating

E-Business 12.2

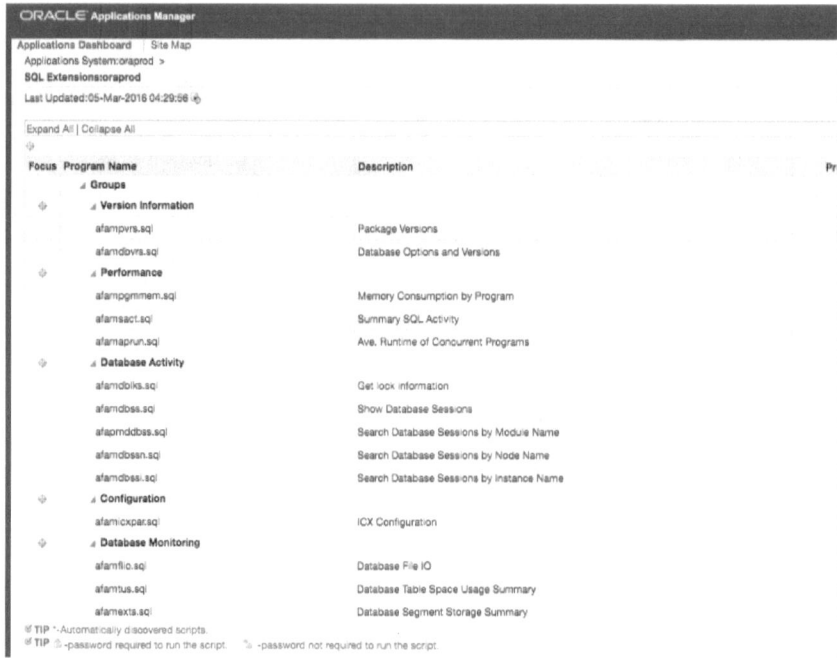

Select from the following Available Database Session Details:
Version Information   **Performance**   **Database Activity**
Configuration   **Database Monitoring**

Run Report

CHAPTER 4
E-BUSINESS SUITE 11I TO 12.2.5 -- OAM PERFORMANCE MONITORING – FORMS SESSIONS

OAM: Oracle Application Manager is an Oracle E-Business Suite Seeded Responsibility. The Oracle Application Manager Seeded Performance Monitoring Screens can be used to monitor, trace and terminate Oracle E-Business Suite Forms Sessions.

Special Note:

- Since the E-Business Suite ICX (Internet Connections) are recorded in the ICX Tables, you can examine the ICX Connections that are current and/or historical. Additionally, the ICX history is available until the Concurrent Request: *Purge Inactive Sessions* is executed and the ICX activity is purged.

- The Forms-Connections, on the other hand, are only available when they are active. So, when a Forms User disconnects, the form information will no longer show a User with an open Forms Session.

- **Profile Options**
  Sign-On:Audit Level must be set to 'FORM' at the SITE level.

  SQL-Query to identify the E-Business Suite SignOn Audit Level appears on the next page.

Special Note: (Continued)

```
SELECT     ptl.user_profile_option_name   upname,
           pro.profile_option_name        pvname,
           DECODE(val.level_id,
           10001, 'Site',
           10002, 'Application',
           10003, 'Responsibility',
           10004, 'User',
           10005, 'Server',
           10007, 'SERVRESP',
           'UnDef')                  lvlset,
           DECODE(to_char(val.level_id),
           '10001', ' ',
           '10002', app.application_short_name,
           '10003', rsp.responsibility_key,
           '10005', svr.node_name,
           '10006', org.name,
           '10004', usr.user_name,
           '10007', 'Serv/resp',
            'UnDef')                       vcntxt,
           TO_CHAR(val.last_update_date,'DD-MON-RR') vupdat,
           val.profile_option_value             vvalue
FROM       fnd_profile_options            pro,
           fnd_profile_option_values      val,
           fnd_profile_options_tl ptl,
           fnd_user                       usr,
           fnd_application                app,
           fnd_responsibility             rsp,
           fnd_nodes                      svr,
           hr_operating_units             org
WHERE      pro.profile_option_id = val.profile_option_id (+)
  AND      pro.profile_option_name = ptl.profile_option_name
  AND      ptl.language         = 'US'
  AND      upper(ptl.user_profile_option_name) like
           upper('%Sign-On:Audit Level%')
  AND       usr.user_id (+)           = val.level_value
  AND       rsp.application_id (+)    =
             val.level_value_application_id
  AND       rsp.responsibility_id (+) = val.level_value
  AND       app.application_id (+)    = val.level_value
  AND       svr.node_id (+)           = val.level_value
  AND       org.organization_id (+)   = val.level_value
ORDER BY 1,3,4;
```

User Profile Name	Profile Name	Profile Level	Context	Last Update Date	Profile Value
Sign-On:Audit Level	SIGNONAUDI T:LEVEL	Site		16-AUG-02	D

Note: Sign-On:Audit Level **Profile-Value: D = Form.**

Oracle Application Manager (OAM) -- Forms Session Monitoring/Tracing/Terminating

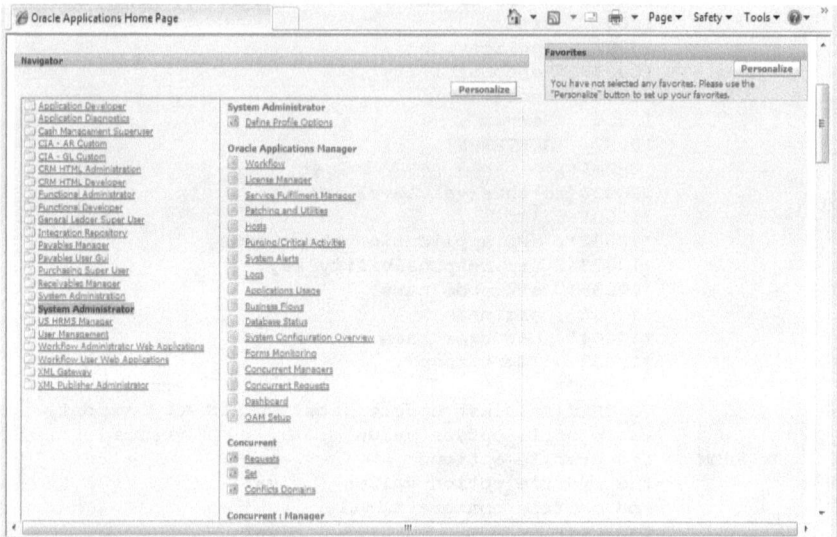

Figure 46 – Oracle Application Manager (OAM) – Forms Monitoring / Tracing / Terminating.

	System Administrator	<Responsibility>
	Oracle Application Manager	<MenuSelections>
	Dashboard	<MenuSelections>

Oracle Application Manager (OAM) -- Forms Session Monitoring/Tracing/Terminating

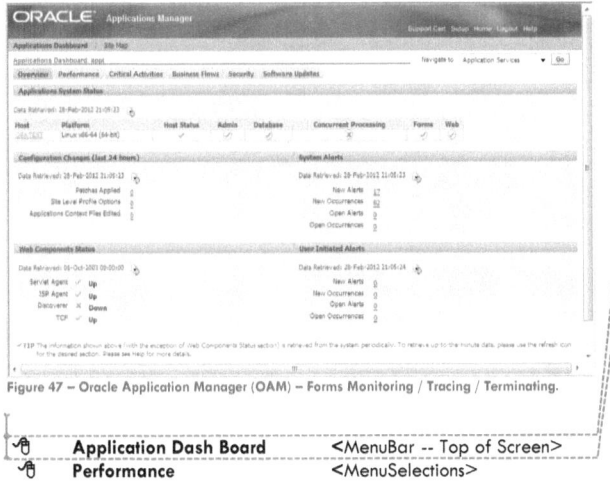

Figure 47 – Oracle Application Manager (OAM) – Forms Monitoring / Tracing / Terminating.

| | **Application Dash Board** | \<MenuBar -- Top of Screen\> |
| | **Performance** | \<MenuSelections\> |

Application Tier Hosts -or- Database Instances:
Forms Sessions

      3   \<Click On The Number of Forms Sessions\>

Comment [B]: Redo this screenshot. When you do the screenshot, reformat the screen and make it narrower so that it will look bigger in the book and be easier to read

Comment [B]: Redo this screenshot. When you do the screenshot, reformat the screen and make it narrower so that it will look bigger in the book and be easier to read

Oracle Application Manager (OAM) -- Forms Session Monitoring/Tracing/Terminating

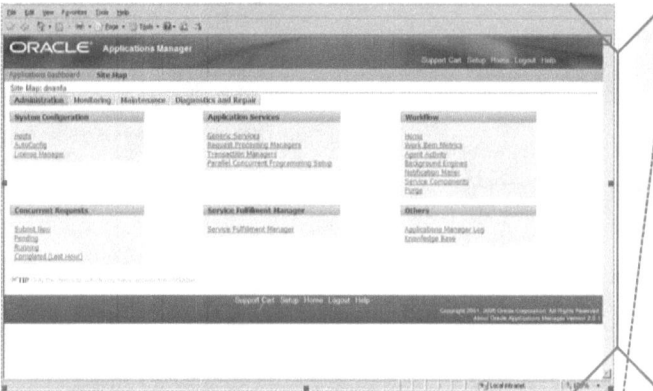

Figure 48 – Oracle Application Manager (OAM) – Forms Monitoring / Tracing / Terminating.

🖱   **Site Map**   <MenuBar -- Top of Screen>
🖱   **Monitoring**   <MenuSelections>

Oracle Application Manager (OAM) — Forms Session Monitoring/Tracing/Terminating

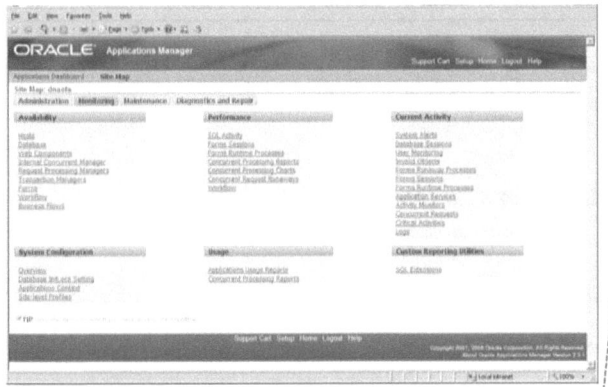

Figure 49 – Oracle Application Manager (OAM) – Forms Monitoring / Tracing / Terminating.

Performance   Middle of Screen
Form Sessions

> **Comment [B]:** Redo this screenshot. When you do the screenshot, reformat the screen and make it narrower so that it will look bigger in the book and be easier to read

Oracle Application Manager (OAM) — Forms Session Monitoring/Tracing/Terminating

Figure 50 – Oracle Application Manager (OAM) – Forms Monitoring / Tracing / Terminating.

🕀 **AUDSID** Select User to be Monitored/Traced/Terminated

🕀 **View All**   <Bottom of Screen/Page>
🕀 **Sort By:**   <Click On the Column-Heading>

Report Columns:

AUDSID	Instance	Machine
Program	Module	User
Process	Status	Log-onTime

Legend:
RTI_PID - Runtime Instance PID <AppsTier OS Process ID)
LRs - Session Logical Reads.
PRs - Session Physical Reads.
CPU - CPU used by this session, seconds.
PGA - Session PGA memory, Kbytes.
UGA - Session UGA memory, Kbytes.
Duration - Time elapsed since activation, hh:mm:ss.

Oracle Application Manager (OAM) -- Forms Session Monitoring/Tracing/Terminating

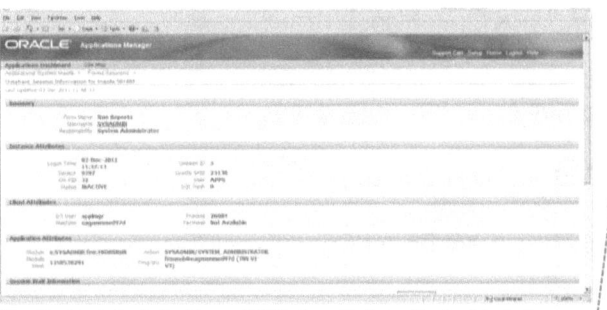

Figure 51 – Oracle Application Manager (OAM) – Forms Monitoring / Tracing / Terminating.

Comment [B]: Redo this screenshot. When you do the screenshot, reformat the screen and make it narrower so that it will look bigger in the book and be easier to read

Summary:
======

Form Name:	Oracle E-Business Suite Current Form-Name
Username:	E-Business Suite User
Responsibility:	E-Business Responsibility

Oracle Application Manager (OAM) -- Forms Session Monitoring/Tracing/Terminating

Instance Attributes: DBTier/Database

Logon Time:	Forms-Session Log-On Time
Serial:	E-Business Suite Database Session Serial#
OS PID:	Unix/Linux Operating System Process ID
Status:	E-Business Suite Database Status (ACTIVE/INACTIVE/KILLED/etc)
Session ID:	E-Business Suite Database Session ID
Oracle SPID:	E-Business Suite DBTier OS Process ID
User:	APPS
SQL Hash	E-Business Suite Database SQL-Statement (Currently Executing SQL-Statement).
Optional: DBTier:	To Manually Kill the Oracle Database Session: Unix/Linux Command: sqlplus / as sysdba ALTER SYSTEM KILL SESSION 'Session ID, Session Serial#'

Oracle Application Manager (OAM) -- Forms Session Monitoring/Tracing/Terminating

Client Attributes: DBTier/Database

OS User:	Forms-Session Log-On Time
Machine:	AppsTier Server-Name
Process:	AppsTier Unix-Process-ID
Terminal:	AppsTier Terminal-Name

AppsTier:
Unix/Linux Command: kill -15 Unix-Process-ID

Application Attributes: Form/Module

Module:	Form Name (Short Name)
Module Hash:	Module Hash
Action:	Module
Program:	Program that is executing this SQL.

Oracle Application Manager (OAM) -- Forms Session Monitoring/Tracing/Terminating

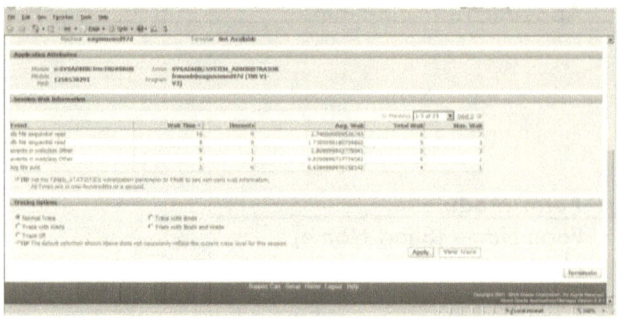

Figure 52 – Oracle Application Manager (OAM) – Forms Monitoring / Tracing / Terminating.

🖰   **Trace with Binds and Waits**
🖰   **Apply**
-or-
🖰   **Terminate.**   **Terminate/Kill the Selected Forms Session.**

CHAPTER 5
E-BUSINESS SUITE 11I TO 12.2.5 -- OAM PERFORMANCE MONITORING – CONCURRENT REQUESTS

OAM: Oracle Application Manager is an Oracle E-Business Suite Seeded Responsibility. The Oracle Application Manager Seeded Performance Monitoring Screens can be used to monitor, trace and terminate Oracle E-Business Suite Concurrent-Processing Sessions.

Special Note:

- Since the E-Business Suite ICX (Internet Connections) are recorded in the ICX Tables, you can examine the ICX Connections that are current and/or historical. Additionally, the ICX history is available until the Concurrent Request: *Purge Inactive Sessions* is executed and the ICX activity is purged.

- The Forms-Connections, on the other hand, are only available when they are active. So, when a Forms User disconnects, the form information will no longer show a User with an open Forms Session.

- **Profile Options**
  Sign-On:Audit Level must be set to 'FORM' at the SITE level.

  SQL-Query to identify the E-Business Suite SignOn Audit Level appears on the next page.

Special Note: (Continued)

```
SELECT      ptl.user_profile_option_name  upname,
            pro.profile_option_name        pvname,
            DECODE(val.level_id,
            10001, 'Site',
            10002, 'Application',
            10003, 'Responsibility',
            10004, 'User',
            10005, 'Server',
            10007, 'SERVRESP',
            'UnDef')                   lvlset,
            DECODE(to_char(val.level_id),
            '10001', '',
            '10002', app.application_short_name,
            '10003', rsp.responsibility_key,
            '10005', svr.node_name,
            '10006', org.name,
            '10004', usr.user_name,
            '10007', 'Serv/resp',
            'UnDef')                          vcntxt,
            TO_CHAR(val.last_update_date,'DD-MON-RR') vupdat,
            val.profile_option_value          vvalue
FROM        fnd_profile_options            pro,
            fnd_profile_option_values      val,
            fnd_profile_options_tl ptl,
            fnd_user                       usr,
            fnd_application                app,
            fnd_responsibility             rsp,
            fnd_nodes                      svr,
            hr_operating_units             org
WHERE       pro.profile_option_id = val.profile_option_id (+)
  AND       pro.profile_option_name = ptl.profile_option_name
  AND       ptl.language          = 'US'
  AND       upper(ptl.user_profile_option_name) like
            upper('%Sign-On:Audit Level%')
  AND        usr.user_id (+)          = val.level_value
  AND        rsp.application_id (+)   =
             val.level_value_application_id
  AND        rsp.responsibility_id (+) = val.level_value
  AND        app.application_id (+)   = val.level_value
  AND        svr.node_id (+)          = val.level_value
  AND        org.organization_id (+)  = val.level_value
ORDER BY 1,3,4;
```

User Profile Name	Profile Name	Profile Level	Context	Last Update Date	Profile Value
Sign-On:Audit Level	SIGNONAUDI T:LEVEL	Site		16-AUG-02	D

Note: Sign-On:Audit Level Profile-Value: D = Form.

Oracle Application Manager (OAM) -- Concurrent Processing Session Monitoring/Tracing/Terminating

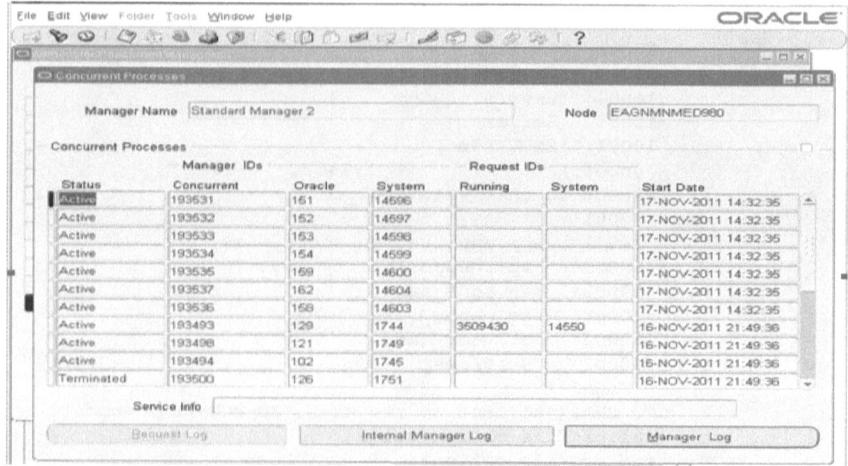

Figure 53 – Oracle Application Manager (OAM) – ConcRequest Monitoring / Tracing / Terminating

 **System Administrator**   <Responsibility>
 **Concurrent Manager**   <MenuSelections>
 **Administrator**   <MenuSelections>
 **Processes**   <MenuSelections>

Oracle Application Manager (OAM) — Concurrent Processing Session Monitoring/Tracing/Terminating

Note: There is ONLY one (1) Active Concurrent-Request: Request-ID "System" ID: 14550

APPSTier: Unix/Linux: ps -efa | grep 14550

```
applmgr  14550  1744  0 14:32 ?           00:00:02
/u00shared/apps/10.1.2/bin/rwrun
mode=character P_CONC_REQUEST_ID=3509430 p_from_date='2014/06/01
00:00:00' p_to_date='
00:00:00' p_include_feeder='Y' p_incl_etrv='Y' p_sample_size='100'
report=/a00shared/ap/reports/US/XXAPAUDIT.rdf userid=APPS batch=yes
destype=file
desname=/a00shared/APPLCSF/out/o3509430.outdesformat=/u00shared/app
s/appl/fnd/12.0.0/
reports/HPW pagesize=180x66
```

Oracle Application Manager (OAM) -- Concurrent Processing Session Monitoring/Tracing/Terminating

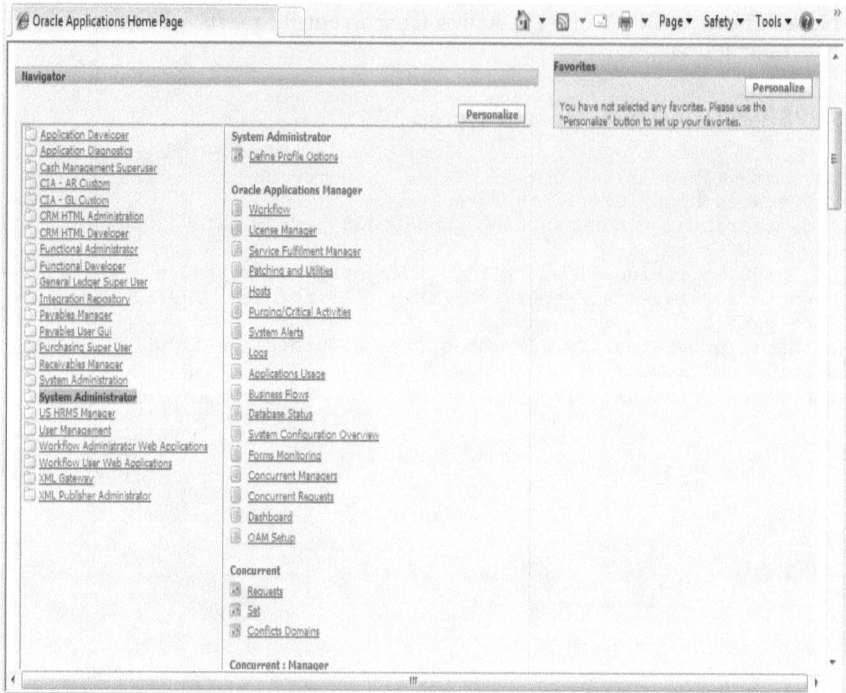

Figure 54 – Oracle Application Manager (OAM) – ConcRequest Monitoring / Tracing / Terminating

🖱 **System Administrator**   <Responsibility>
🖱 **Oracle Application Manager**   <MenuSelections>

Oracle Application Manager (OAM) -- Concurrent Processing Session Monitoring/Tracing/Terminating

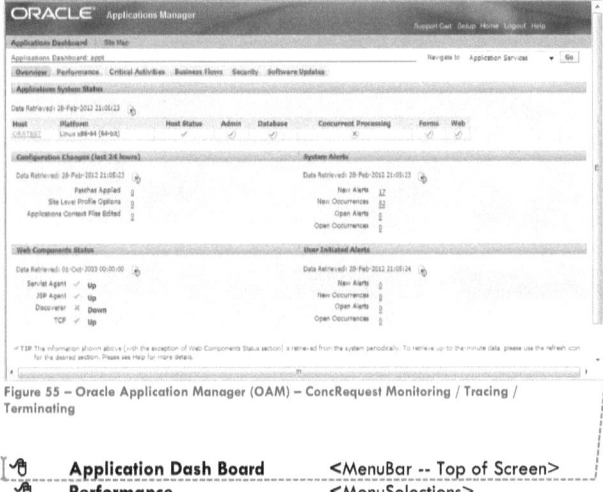

Figure 55 – Oracle Application Manager (OAM) – ConcRequest Monitoring / Tracing / Terminating

| | **Application Dash Board** | <MenuBar -- Top of Screen> |
| | **Performance** | <MenuSelections> |

Application Tier Hosts -or- Database Instances:
Concurrent Processing Sessions
           <u>3</u>   <Click On The Number of Concurrent Sessions>

Oracle Application Manager (OAM) -- Concurrent Processing Session Monitoring/Tracing/Terminating

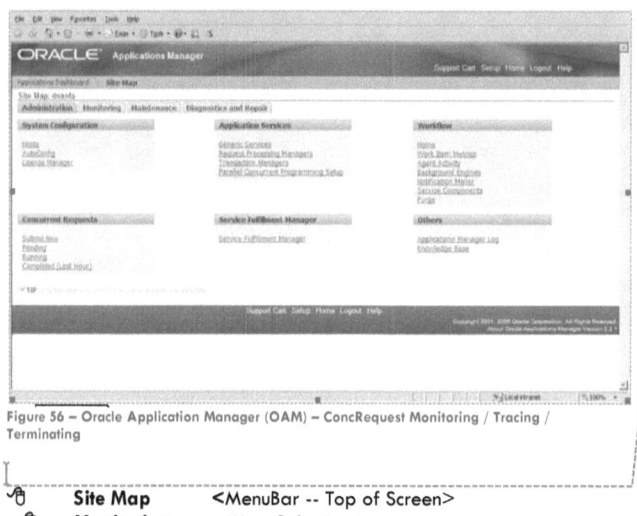

Figure 56 – Oracle Application Manager (OAM) – ConcRequest Monitoring / Tracing / Terminating

🖱 **Site Map**   <MenuBar -- Top of Screen>
🖱 **Monitoring**   <MenuSelections>

Oracle Application Manager (OAM) -- Concurrent Processing Session Monitoring/Tracing/Terminating

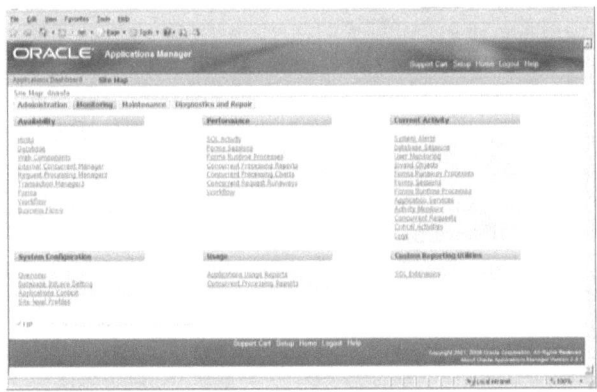

Figure 57 – Oracle Application Manager (OAM) – ConcRequest Monitoring / Tracing / Terminating

Performance   <MenuBar -- Top of Screen>
Concurrent Processing Reports <Menu Selections>

Comment [B]: Redo this screenshot. When you do the screenshot, reformat the screen and make it narrower so that it will look bigger in the book and be easier to read

ABOUT THE AUTHORS

Bill Dunham (*Oracle Ace*)

Bill is the founder and principal owner of OATC, Inc. He is a well known Oracle Applications and Technology consultant, having worked with Oracle products since 1985, and Oracle EBS Apps since 1991 (MPL7➜R12). His extensive experience with EBS Applications and Technology makes him a trusted advisor to many clients throughout the US and Europe. Bill has worked in many IT and project capacities over the years, mostly focusing as an EBS Program/Project Manager, Architect, Technical/Functional Lead, QA Manager and client advocate. Bill has presented papers at many local and regional Oracle Application Users Group (OAUG) events and at Oracle OpenWorld (OOW). Bill has authored articles for OAUG INSIGHT magazine, as well as co-authored two books, "Special Edition Using Oracle Applications" and "Special Edition Using Oracle 11i" and is co-authoring this new book series called *Oracle EBS Applications StreetSmarts*®. Bill has designed, developed and authored papers on the "CRP Method" for enterprise application projects. This method focuses on critical and core project activities, all while reducing project costs and focusing on client success. Bill is a member of the Oracle EBS Applications Technology Customer Advisory Board (CAB) for Oracle Corporation, Coordinator for ESOAUG, member of the OAUG GEO/SIG Board, Director on the OAUG Board of Directors, and an Oracle Applications & Applications Technology ACE.

Michael Barone (*Oracle Ace Nominee*)

Michael is an Oracle E-Business Suite Database Administrator with 25 years of IT experience and 16 years of Oracle Applications DBA experience including RAC (Real Application Cluster), ASM (Automatic Storage Management), and Oracle Applications (E-Business Suite). Michael's experience includes full cycle installations and upgrades as well as architecture, installation, administration, upgrade and development of Oracle relational databases. Most recently, Michael has installed, set up, upgraded and administered the production, test, and development databases for major international organizations, federal / state / local government agencies, and manufacturers of hospital equipment, oil-and-gas distribution, automotive-subassemblies, landscape-equipment, diesel-engines, jet-engine turbine blades, medical-equipment, pharmaceuticals, aluminum, concrete, wire and steel products. Michael speaks regularly at Oracle Open World and Oracle Application Users Group (OAUG) Conferences and Regional Oracle Users Group (OUG) Conferences.

ENJOY THE WHOLE SERIES!

Stay tuned for our next books in the **StreetSmarts**® series. Out intentions are to release the initial draft of these books and provide subsequent updates as new information is released or we feel like releasing a new version! This is the planned release order at this time (subject to change):

1. Oracle E-Business Suite StreetSmarts® What Scripts (version 5.0)
2. Oracle E-Business Suite StreetSmarts® Unix/Linux Menus (version 4.0)
3. **Oracle E-Business Suite StreetSmarts® Performance Monitoring (version 2.0)**
4. Oracle E-Business Suite StreetSmarts® Functional Analyzers
5. Oracle E-Business Suite StreetSmarts® ADOP On-line Patching ADZD Scripts
6. Oracle E-Business Suite StreetSmarts® CRP Method [Fall 2016]
7. Oracle E-Business Suite StreetSmarts® AutoConfig
8. Oracle E-Business Suite StreetSmarts® Cloning
9. Oracle E-Business Suite StreetSmarts® Upgrades
10. Oracle E-Business Suite StreetSmarts® Purging & Archiving [NEW]

More information is available at:

http://www.oatcinc.com

Check out our new logos!

www.ingramcontent.com/pod-product-compliance
Lightning Source LLC
Chambersburg PA
CBHW022104170526
45157CB00004B/1476